WRITING AND SCHOOL REFORM: WRITING INSTRUCTION IN THE AGE OF COMMON CORE AND STANDARDIZED TESTING

T0099494

PERSPECTIVES ON WRITING
Series Editors, Susan H. McLeod and Rich Rice

The Perspectives on Writing series addresses writing studies in a broad sense. Consistent with the wide ranging approaches characteristic of teaching and scholarship in writing across the curriculum, the series presents works that take divergent perspectives on working as a writer, teaching writing, administering writing programs, and studying writing in its various forms.

The WAC Clearinghouse, Colorado State University Open Press, and University Press of Colorado are collaborating so that these books will be widely available through free digital distribution and low-cost print editions. The publishers and the Series editors are committed to the principle that knowledge should freely circulate. We see the opportunities that new technologies have for further democratizing knowledge. And we see that to share the power of writing is to share the means for all to articulate their needs, interest, and learning into the great experiment of literacy.

Recent Books in the Series

Lisa Emerson, *The Forgotten Tribe: Scientists as Writers* (2017)

Jacob S. Blumner and Pamela B, Childers (Eds.), *WAC Partnerships Between Secondary and Postsecondary Institutio*ns (2015)

Nathan Shepley, *Placing the History of College Writing: Stories from the Incomplete Archive* (2015)

Asao B. Inoue, *Antiracist Writing Assessment Ecologies: An Approach to Teaching and Assessing Writing for a Socially Just Future* (2015)

Theresa Lillis, Kathy Harrington, Mary R. Lea, and Sally Mitchell (Eds.), *Working with Academic Literacies: Case Studies Towards Transformative Practice* (2015)

Beth L. Hewett and Kevin Eric DePew (Eds.), *Foundational Practices of Online Writing Instruction* (2015)

Christy I. Wenger, *Yoga Minds, Writing Bodies: Contemplative Writing Pedagogy* (2015)

Sarah Allen, *Beyond Argument: Essaying as a Practice of (Ex)Change* (2015)

Steven J. Corbett, *Beyond Dichotomy: Synergizing Writing Center and Classroom Pedagogies* (2015)

Tara Roeder and Roseanne Gatto (Eds.), *Critical Expressivism: Theory and Practice in the Composition Classroom* (2014)

WRITING AND SCHOOL REFORM: WRITING INSTRUCTION IN THE AGE OF COMMON CORE AND STANDARDIZED TESTING

Joanne Addison and Sharon James McGee

The WAC Clearinghouse
wac.colostate.edu
Fort Collins, Colorado

University Press of Colorado
www.upcolorado.com
Boulder, Colorado

The WAC Clearinghouse, Fort Collins, Colorado 80523-1040

University Press of Colorado, Boulder, Colorado 80303

Printed in the United States of America

Library of Congress Cataloging-in-Publication Data

Names: Addison, Joanne, author. | McGee, Sharon James, author.
Title: Writing and school reform : writing instruction in the age of Common Core and stan-
   dardized testing / Joanne Addison and Sharon James McGee.
Other titles: Perspectives on writing (Fort Collins, Colo.)
Description: Fort Collins, Colo. : WAC Clearinghouse ; Boulder, Colorado : University Press of
   Colorado, [2016] | Series: Perspectives on writing | Includes bibliographical references.
Identifiers: LCCN 2016045020 | ISBN 9781607326458 (pbk.) | ISBN 9781607326465 (ebook)
Subjects: LCSH: English language—Writing—Study and teaching (Higher)—United States—
   Evaluation. | Educational accountability—United States—History. | Educational tests and
   measurements—United States—History. | Common Core State Standards (Education)
Classification: LCC PE1405.U6 A34 2016 | DDC 808/.042071073—dc23
LC record available at https://lccn.loc.gov/2016045020

Copyeditor: Julia Smth
Designer: Mike Palmquist
Series Editors: Susan H. McLeod and Rich Rice

This book is printed on acid-free paper.

This book includes chapters based in part on the following publications:

Addison, Joanne, and Sharon James McGee. "Writing in high school/writing in college: Research trends and future directions." *College Composition and Communication* 62.1 (2010): 147–179. Copyright © 2010 by the National Council of Teachers of English. Used with permission.

Addison, Joanne, and Sharon James McGee. "To the Core: College Composition Classrooms in The Age of Accountability, Standardized Testing, and Common Core State Standards." *Rhetoric Review* 34.2 (2015): 200–218. Copyright © 2015 Joanne Addison and Sharon James McGee.

The WAC Clearinghouse supports teachers of writing across the disciplines. Hosted by Colorado State University, and supported by the Colorado State Univeristy Open Press, it brings together scholarly journals and book series as well as resources for teachers who use writing in their courses. This book is available in digital formats for free download at wac.colostate.edu.

Founded in 1965, the University Press of Colorado is a nonprofit cooperative publishing enterprise supported, in part, by Adams State University, Colorado State University, Fort Lewis College, Metropolitan State University of Denver, Regis University, University of Colorado, University of Northern Colorado, Utah State University, and Western State Colorado University. For more information, visit www.upcolorado.com.

CONTENTS

Contents

WRITING AND SCHOOL REFORM: WRITING INSTRUCTION IN THE AGE OF COMMON CORE AND STANDARDIZED TESTING

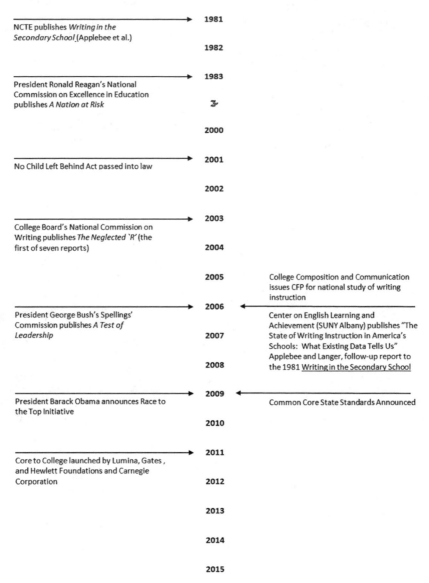

1981	NCTE publishes *Writing in the Secondary School* (Applebee et al.)	
1982		
1983	President Ronald Reagan's National Commission on Excellence in Education publishes *A Nation at Risk*	
⅔		
2000		
2001	No Child Left Behind Act passed into law	
2002		
2003	College Board's National Commission on Writing publishes *The Neglected 'R'* (the first of seven reports)	
2004		
2005		College Composition and Communication issues CFP for national study of writing instruction
2006	President George Bush's Spellings' Commission publishes *A Test of Leadership*	Center on English Learning and Achievement (SUNY Albany) publishes "The State of Writing Instruction in America's Schools: What Existing Data Tells Us" Applebee and Langer, follow-up report to the 1981 Writing in the Secondary School
2007		
2008		
2009	President Barack Obama announces Race to the Top Initiative	Common Core State Standards Announced
2010		
2011	Core to College launched by Lumina, Gates, and Hewlett Foundations and Carnegie Corporation	
2012		
2013		
2014		
2015		

A timeline of movement toward testing and accountability and away from best practices and standards

INTRODUCTION

At a 2004 venture-capitalist meeting in California, Stanford economist Paul Romer reminded us: "A crisis is a terrible thing to waste" (qtd. in Rosenthal). He was talking about an educational crisis related to the perceived competition the United States was facing as educational levels rose in other countries. Since that time, numerous headlines have pointed to a national crisis in education:

> "U.S. Could Fall Behind in Global 'Brain Race'" (*USA Today*, February 8, 2006)
>
> "In Test, Few Students Are Proficient Writers" (*New York Times*, April 3, 2008)
>
> "Study: College Students Not Learning Much" (*CBS News. com*, January 18, 2011)
>
> "American Students Fall in International Academic Tests, Chinese Lead the Pack" (*U.S. News and World Report*, December 3, 2013)

Social critics and educational researchers have questioned the validity of our many educational crises over the years—crises that have required the expenditure of much political and monetary capital in order to manufacture consent around the need for unprecedented amounts of standardized testing and accountability, as well as major educational initiatives such as the No Child Left Behind (NCLB) Act and, more recently, the Common Core State Standards (CCSS). The movement toward testing and accountability and away from best practices and standards is eroding teacher and student agency as greater measures of control over our classrooms are enacted. Understanding the origins of these crises, as well as their effects on writing instruction, is a crucial step toward charting a path forward that reasserts teacher and student agency in the research and practice of writing instruction and assessment.

One well-known effort to counter the most recent crisis can be found in the work of David Berliner and Bruce J. Biddle's *The Manufactured Crisis: Myths, Fraud, and the Attack on America's Public Schools*. This best-selling book counters myths surrounding America's schools and student achievement, including:

- Declining student achievement in U.S. primary schools
- Falling performance among U.S. college students
- Falling status of U.S. schools compared with schools in other countries

3

- Deficient productivity of U.S. workers tied to inadequate training received in U.S. schools
- U.S. production of far too few scientists, mathematicians, and engineers, resulting in industrial leadership losses
- Inadequately qualified teaching staff in U.S. schools (5–6)

Berliner and Biddle contend that none of these myths are supported by a careful collection and analysis of available data, and they set out to prove that these charges against public education in the United States are false. More recently, Berliner renewed his efforts in his 2014 book, co-authored with Gene V. Glass, *50 Myths and Lies that Threaten America's Public Schools: The Real Crisis in Education.*

In both books the authors address charges that U.S. students are falling behind, especially when compared to students in other countries. These charges, they claim, are based on a presentation of data to the U.S. public that is incomplete and misleading, not the careful and thoughtful analysis that should be used to chart a path for our educational policies and practices. For example, in *50 Myths and Lies that Threaten America's Public Schools* the authors point out that following the release of the 2009 Programme for International Student Assessment (PISA) test scores, national media sources declared: "Wake-Up Call: U.S. Students Trail Global Leaders" and "Competitors Still Beat U.S. in Tests." "The frenzied media attention given to international test results, ranking countries from best to worst, has been supported by commentary from apparent experts like U.S. Secretary of Education Arne Duncan, who said the 2009 PISA test results were an 'absolute wake-up call for America,' showing that 'we have to deal with the brutal truth' and get much more serious about investing in education" (*50 Myths,* 12–13).

Berliner and others rely on the work of Gerald Bracey, former director of research, evaluation, and testing for the Virginia Department of Education (1977–1986), fellow at the Education Policy Studies Laboratory at Arizona State University, and author of books such as *Reading Educational Research: How to Avoid Getting Educationally Snookered,* to help dispel this myth of low comparative achievement:

> Many critics cite the performance of American students on
> international comparisons of mathematics and science. The
> most often used comparison comes from rankings on the
> Programme for International Student Assessment (PISA),
> from the Organization for Economic Cooperation and Development (OECD). . . . It should be noted that these rankings
> are determined by nations' average scores. . . . A publication

from OECD itself observes that if one examines the number of highest-scoring students in science, the United States has 25% of all high-scoring students in the world. . . . The picture emerging from this highest-scorer comparison is far different than that suggested by the frequently cited national average comparisons; it is a picture that suggests many American schools are actually doing very well indeed . . . it is only when we look beyond the mean and consider the distribution of students and schools that we see the true picture. Students attending American schools run the gamut from excellent to poor. Well-resourced schools serving wealthy neighborhoods are showing excellent results. Poorly resourced schools serving low-income communities of color do far worse. (Bracey, *The Bracey Report on the Condition of Public Education* 2–3)

According to the OECD itself, among nations with high average scores, the U.S. actually outperforms Japan, Korea, Taipei, Finland, and Hong Kong. As Bracey, Berliner, and others argue, the problem is not a relatively new decline in student achievement requiring a wake-up call. The problem is that students living in poverty in the United States, and especially students of color living in the United States, continue to underperform their wealthier peers. It is no wonder, then, that *on average*, a country like Finland that has a child poverty rate of less than 5 percent, scores better on PISA than a country like the United States where the child poverty rate often exceeds 20 percent. The perpetuation of this myth of comparative decline is also taken up by Patrick Shannon, Anne Elrod Whitney, and Maja Wilson in their discussion of the ways CCSS are being framed by corporations and private testing companies in order to sell them to the public ("Framing").

If the problem really is one of poverty and wealth distribution in the United States, and not overall levels of academic achievement, why manufacture an educational crisis and create widespread concern and even panic about our educational system as a whole? The cynical among us would argue that there's not much money to be made off poverty. But America's educational system as a whole is a multi-billion dollar enterprise from which those with the needed capital and political support can profit. As Jonathan Zimmerman, an educational historian at New York University, quips, "When the federal government starts doing things like requiring all states to test all kids, there's going to be gold in those hills" (as qtd in S. Simon). Through this lens, we can see how the serious investment in education called for by Secretary of Education Arne Duncan and others has led largely to investment in private testing companies. Because these companies realize, as Paul Romer reminded us, you never want a crisis to go to waste, especially, we would add, one that has been manufactured with the potential for huge profits.

We can look at the publishing company Pearson as a case in point. According to the article "No Profit Left Behind"—based on a review of Pearson's contracts, business plans, email exchanges, tax filings, lobbying reports, and marketing materials—half of its $8 billion dollars in global sales comes from its North American education division (S. Simon). In addition to its command of the textbook industry and online learning in both K–12 and higher education, Pearson dominates the standardized testing market in the United States, maintaining contracts with twenty-one states as well as Washington, New York City, and Puerto Rico (S. Simon). Estimates from the Brookings Institution put Pearson's annual revenue from standardized testing in the K–12 market alone in the United States at $258 million (Chingos). In fact, Pearson has displayed a unique ability to capitalize on the need for standardized tests as mandated by the No Child Left Behind Act, Race to the Top funding initiative, and implementation of Common Core State Standards. And, of course, to prepare students for Pearson exams, schools can buy Pearson textbooks, workbooks, test preparation books, online tutoring services, learning management systems, and teacher consultants. From this standpoint, it seems that Pearson is writing the curriculum, training the teachers, and designing the tests, all at a huge profit.

But Pearson is currently experiencing significant backlash—much of it from former and current Partnership for Assessment of Readiness for College and Careers (PARCC) member states. In the spring of 2010, twenty-three states and the District of Columbia joined PARCC. As of the spring of 2015, only eleven states and the District of Columbia remain PARCC members. Pearson signed a contract with PARCC to develop and administer standardized tests tied to the Common Core State Standards in all member states. So problematic has this effort been that in June of 2014 the Bill and Melinda Gates Foundation called for a two-year moratorium on enacting negative consequences for teachers and students based on standardized tests related to CCSS (Rich); Pearson is in the midst of a bid-rigging lawsuit; and in some school districts in PARCC member states, the opposition from parents and students has threatened the ground upon which these tests stand. A promising example is that of Fairview High School students in Boulder, CO (which happens to be the home school of one of the authors of this book). Colorado is one of the PARCC member states. In November of 2014, only 7 out of 538 seniors at Fairview High School took the test as the others protested the new testing requirement (Garcia).

Perhaps as Grover Whitehurst, former director of the Institute of Education Sciences (IES) within the U.S. Department of Education and current senior fellow at the Brookings Institution, suggests in his article "The Future of Test-Based Accountability:"

> we're in a transformative period fueled by a kind of restlessness that nobody is getting accountability right, the achievement problem remains, and ideas are not manifold about what to do next. At some point the prevailing standards and accountability approach to education reform will be replaced with new designs that are more productive, or at least different.

Further, as Patrick Shannon suggests, we might view the Common Core State Standards as "a value-laden, open project in continuous development—just waiting for teachers, parents, and students to step forward in order to negotiate their design as well as their enactment in classrooms" (3).

It is not our primary intent in this book to support or challenge arguments concerning the most recent manufactured crisis in education—Bracey, Berliner, Shannon, Wilson and others have and continue to do so in more depth than we can in the space of this volume. Whether the most recent crisis, as well as the crises that came before, are manufactured or not, they result in serious material consequences for writing instruction. This is increasingly true not only in our K–12 classrooms, but in higher education as well. Because for better or worse, the Common Core State Standards "have made writing and the teaching of writing an integral part of the school reform movement . . . provid[ing] benchmarks for a variety of writing skills and applications students are expected to master at each grade and across grades" (Graham et al. 879), within traditional language arts classrooms as well as across the curriculum. CCSS and their attendant high-stakes standardized tests will certainly have an effect on the ways students enter our writing classrooms, as these tests have been clearly linked to "changing the nature of teaching, narrowing the curriculum, and limiting student learning" ("How Standardized Tests Shape—and Limit—Student Learning"). It is our intent to understand the positive and negative consequences for those of us concerned with writing instruction—teachers, students, professional organizations, administrators, researchers, policy makers, and others—and respond to the perceived literacy crisis on multiple levels.

§

In the spring of 2006, the Conference on College Composition and Communication issued a call for proposals to study the types of writing American students do in high school and college. This is the same year that a collaborative report issued by the National Writing Project, the College Board, and the Center on English Learning and Achievement called for a large-scale study of schools across the United States in order to better understand the current state of writing instruction in the nation. Shortly thereafter, the Consortium for the Study of Writing in College, a joint effort between the National Survey of Student Engagement and the Council of Writing Program Administrators, emerged in part to "create a national portrait of the ways writing is used in four-year colleges and universities in the United States" (Anderson, Anson, Gonyea, and Paine). These research efforts came on the heels of several reports issued by the National Commission on Writing and others stating that writing instruction in the United States had gone largely ignored and that students and recent graduates were increasingly unprepared for writing tasks in both school and the workplace.

Why does it seem that in 2006 our profession lacked sufficient collective knowledge of the types and quality of writing instruction in U.S. schools as reports of the demise of writing skills began to proliferate? Have we, as a profession, paid enough attention to how state and federal governments, private testing companies, deep-pocketed granting agencies, and large corporations have framed these reports and how they have begun to claim unprecedented power and authority over the work of faculty and students? And, what does this mean for writing instruction now and in the future?

The answers are, of course, quite complicated. We could start by looking at departments of English since most writing at the university level remains in their domain. And departments of English continue to privilege reading over writing. These are the issues Peter Elbow takes up in his article "The War Between Reading and Writing:"

> Of course writing is assigned in a fair number of courses
> (though some students in large universities learn to avoid
> much writing for their whole college career). But when
> writing is assigned, it is traditionally meant to serve reading:
> to summarize, interpret, explain, or make integrations and
> comparisons among readings. In the last couple of years,
> there has even been a widespread move to change the first-
> year writing course into a reading-and-writing course, even
> though it is usually the only writing course—the only place
> in the entire curriculum where writing is emphasized more
> than reading. In every other course in the university, reading
> is privileged, and writing, when used at all, is used to serve
> reading. (10)

There has been some positive change on this front, perhaps most notably by those working in the Writing Across the Curriculum movement, but not enough has changed to suggest that the reading/writing hierarchy has even come close to being leveled.

The privileging of reading over writing is not just a matter of English Department debates. For example, the No Child Left Behind Act further enshrined the reading/writing hierarchy and the entailments that followed. A brief history of NCLB can help us understand how it so forcefully compelled our nation to focus on test scores in reading and math to the exclusion of all else. While NCLB is most often thought to have been a signature policy of President George W. Bush's administration, its foundation was firmly established in the early 1980s, during President Ronald Regan's administration, with the publication of *A Nation at Risk*. The drafting of this report was commissioned by the U.S. Department of Education with the charge to "review and synthesize the data and scholarly literature on the quality of learning and teaching in the nation's schools, colleges, and universities, both public and private, with special concern for the education experience of teen-age youth" (39). In the end, the authors found that existing educational practices put nothing less than fundamental ideals of U.S. society at risk:

> Part of what is at risk is the promise first made on this
> continent: All, regardless of race or class or economic status,
> are entitled to a fair chance and to the tools for developing
> their individual powers of mind and spirit to the utmost.
> This promise means that all children by virtue of their own
> efforts, competently guided, can hope to attain the mature
> and informed judgment needed to secure gainful employ-
> ment, and to manage their own lives, thereby serving not
> only their own interest but also the progress of society itself.
> (*Nation* 8)

Tapping into the collective fear that arises when our cultural narratives of the "American Dream" and the "Common Good" are threatened, the authors of *A Nation at Risk* advocate for educational reform in many areas. For example, they advocate for the adoption of the New Basics curriculum in which all students should receive in-depth instruction. These basics include English (explicitly including writing), math, science, social studies, and to a lesser extent, computer science (24). Despite the relatively broad scope of their recommendations, the one recommendation in *A Nation at Risk* that perseveres is "Standards and Expectations":

> Standardized tests of achievement (not to be confused with aptitude tests) should be administered at major transition points from one level of schooling to another and particularly from high school to college or work. The purposes of these tests would be to: (a) certify the student's credentials; (b) identify the need for remedial intervention; and (c) identify the opportunity for advanced or accelerated work. The tests should be administered as part of a nationwide (but not Federal) system of State and local standardized tests. This system should include other diagnostic procedures that assist teachers and students to evaluate student progress. (28)

Clearly, the authors of *A Nation at Risk* intended for students to be tested in all five of the New Basics. Perhaps more importantly, they also intended for there to be a system of state and local tests that are used in conjunction with other means of assessing student progress. But, these recommendations were drastically diluted and very narrowly interpreted when acted upon in the No Child Left Behind Act. Through NCLB, academic achievement is defined primarily in terms of reading and math scores on standardized tests. Perhaps more important is that NCLB marks the first step toward an unprecedented emphasis on accountability and testing through punitive measures that forced schools to expend so much of their effort and money on improving math and reading scores that little time and money was left for other subjects.

While it took some time for No Child Left Behind to grow out of *A Nation at Risk*, it has taken relatively little time for the law to unravel. NCLB was passed in 2001 and implemented in 2002. By 2006, however, its effects were widespread and becoming increasingly clear. In 2006 the Center on Education Policy conducted a survey of 299 school districts in fifty states, along with case studies of thirty-eight diverse districts and forty-two schools. Among the center's findings was a pervasive narrowing of the curriculum in 71 percent of the school districts as they increased time spent on reading and math while minimizing and even eliminating other subjects. This narrowing of the curriculum, designed to ensure schools would meet the Adequate Yearly Progress (AYP) benchmarks required by NCLB as evidenced by test scores in reading and math, continues today. Despite this testing mandate, a number of recent research reports show no significant increase in reading ability on multiple measures. For example, the U.S. Department of Education's National Center for Education Statistics found that in the National Assessment of Educational Progress's 2009 results, there was only a slight increase in the reading scores of fourth and eighth graders from 1992–2007 (*The Nation's Report Card: Reading 2009*) and no significant increase from 2007 to 2009, when we would expect to see some of the greatest gains as a result of NCLB.

Perhaps the best way to understand the unraveling of NCLB is through the stories of major architects and once staunch supporters of the law who have become so disillusioned by its effects that they are now actively working against it. One fairly well-known story is that of Diane Ravitch, a research professor of education at New York University as well as a senior fellow at the Brookings Institution. From 1991 to 1993 she was the assistant secretary of education under George H. W. Bush, and one of the prime movers in the testing, accountability, choice, and free market approach to education that are the hallmarks of NCLB. As described by Arthur Levine, former president of Teacher's College and current president of the Woodrow Wilson National Fellowship Foundation, Diane Ravitch "has done more than anyone I can think of in America to drive home the message of accountability and charters and testing" (qtd. in Dillon, "Scholar's School Reform U-Turn Shakes Up Debate").

In Ravitch's 2010 account of NCLB, *The Death and Life of the Great American School System*, she describes the intellectual crisis she experienced related to the educational reform movement that led to NCLB: "Where once I had been hopeful, even enthusiastic, about the potential benefits of testing, accountability, choice and markets, I now found myself experiencing profound doubts about these same ideas" (1). She continues, characterizing the implementation of NCLB as a "hijacking" of the standards movement:

> Although it [NCLB] is often claimed as a natural outgrowth
> of the standards movement, it was not. It demanded that
> schools generate higher test scores in basic skills, but it
> required no curriculum at all, nor did it raise standards. It
> ignored such important studies as history, civics, literature,
> science, the arts, and geography. (16)

Ravitch now describes NCLB as the "Death Star" of U.S. education, something that cannot be fixed and that must be abandoned ("NCLB: The Death Star of American Education").

As much as we agree with Ravitch's assessment of the destructive effects of NCLB, we need to point out that the "basic skills" being tested by NCLB as required for federal reporting include only reading and math. Further, Ravitch's list of forgotten studies also forgets an important area of study—writing—not writing as it serves history, civics, literature, and other subjects, but writing as a subject in and of itself.

The fact that NCLB required measures of student performance in only reading and math drew significant criticism and created an opening for private testing companies. For example, shortly after the bill became law, College Board created the National Commission on Writing. While College Board acknowledges that "the decision to create the commission was animated in part by the Board's plans to offer a writing assessment in 2005 as part of the new SAT," they also claim "the larger motivation lay in the growing concern within education, business, and policy-making communities that the level of writing in the United States is not what it should be" *(The Neglected R* 10). This claim was used to authorize a series of reports by College Board showing just how dismal our writing skills have become, arguing for improved practices and, of course, justifying the need for even more standardized tests such as theirs.

Much closer to home for many of us in higher education, this issue became a matter of national debate again when "On March 2, President Obama signed a bill eliminating direct federal funding for the National Writing Project (NWP), the nation's leading effort to improve writing and learning in the digital age" (Washington). Importantly, the National Writing Project is a federally funded program that truly believed in and supported teachers and their agency. This cut was made at the same time that President Obama began arguing for a historic $4 billion to fund his Race to the Top initiative. Obviously, eliminating funding for NWP was not simply a matter of fiscal crisis, as legislators and policymakers would have us believe, but rather a logical culminating event on the road to testing and accountability wherein private testing companies are subsidized and largely unregulated by the federal government. Indeed, as we discuss in Chapters One and Four, while the federal government ultimately restored a small amount of funding to the NWP, many local sites across the United States are now funded in significant part by private foundations such as the Bill and Melinda Gates Foundation in return for their support of the Common Core State Standards, exemplifying the types of entanglements we will work to unravel throughout this book.

§

Let's return to the question of how it came to be that in 2006 the Conference on College Composition and Communication, the National Writing Project, the Center on English Learning and Achievement, and others were issuing calls to study writing instruction in U.S. schools and colleges. It seems that by 2006, Ravitch and other early supporters were fully convinced that NCLB was not raising student achievement and the choice and accountability movements were a grave threat to the U.S. public education system. This is the same year the Center on English Learning and Achievement at the University of Albany, in collaboration with the National Writing Project and the College Board, published

"The State of Writing Instruction in America's Schools: What Existing Data Tells Us." Written by Arthur Applebee and Judith Langer, two well-respected scholars in education, literacy, and writing studies, this report became a launching pad for their National Study of Writing Instruction. This is because, as it turns out, there has been no large-scale, empirical study of writing and writing instruction in the middle and high school years since Applebee's *Writing in the Secondary School,* a study that gathered data in 1979–1980. Thus, we can see that by 2006, the field of writing studies was long overdue for large-scale empirical studies of writing in our high schools and colleges.

We don't want to suggest that no significant work has occurred in this area since Applebee's study in 1979. In recent years, many national surveys have been conducted that primarily measure the *attitudes* of teachers, students, employers, and the general public concerning writing instruction in U.S. schools and colleges. Prominent examples include the national public opinion survey conducted by the National Writing Project, reports issued by the National Commission on Writing (an arm of College Board), and the ACT National Curriculum Survey. While these surveys are useful in helping us understand the felt importance of writing instruction from a very broad perspective, they don't provide us with detailed information concerning what kinds of writing and writing instruction is actually practiced by students and teachers across the curriculum in high schools and colleges throughout the United States.

Notable exceptions exist such as the Harvard Study of Writing, the Stanford Study of Writing, and the Denver Longitudinal Study of Writing. But these projects, while very important, provide a limited picture of writing and writing instruction as they are local in nature and bound by a lack of generalizability beyond elite institutions of higher education. A need existed to determine the kinds of writing undertaken at a diversity of institutions of higher education as well as the high schools that feed into them. With grant support from the Conference on College Composition and Communication, we offered an initial response to this need by conducting research at both the national and local level, gathering direct and indirect evidence, in order to offer an empirically based description of the types of writing and writing instruction students and teachers engage in over the course of a semester. Our final data includes faculty and students from diverse high schools[1] and colleges: one suburban public high school in a relatively affluent neighborhood (27 percent free/reduced lunches and 7 percent dropout rate), one urban public high school in a relatively poor neighborhood (63 percent free/reduced lunches and 26 percent dropout rate), and one private all-girls Catholic high school, as well as two community colleges, two four-year public institutions, one four-year private institution, one public master's-granting institution, and one doctoral-granting, flagship institution.

Participating in our research were 544 faculty and 1,412 students from a wide range of disciplines.

After gathering data, presenting it at conferences, and publishing it, we were still very much drawn to this line of inquiry. As teachers who work with teachers, primarily graduate students who are also teaching in our public school systems, we are reminded on a daily basis of their struggles to meet the demands of our current system of testing, punishment, and reward. As we struggle with them to sort through what is and isn't possible in U.S. classrooms, we continue to be motivated to understand the forces that shape writing instruction in U.S. high schools and colleges. However, we are also motivated by yet another happening in 2006—a trend we thought would fade away but seems to be gathering force as shrinking state budgets are used to justify systems of accountability, punishment, and reward not seen before in higher education and that parallel the path K–12 has been led down by NCLB.

In 2006, the U.S. Secretary of Education's Commission on the Future of Higher Education released its report, *A Test of Leadership: Charting the Future of U.S. Higher Education* (Spellings Commission). Echoing the same threats to the American Dream and the Common Good as *A Nation at Risk*, the new report "urge[s] the creation of a robust culture of accountability and transparency throughout higher education" (20). It names specific standardized tests, such as the Collegiate Learning Assessment, for use in our colleges. Writing in 2007 in response to this effort, Christopher Gallagher notes: "Some believe the machinations of these usual suspects, the famously autonomous culture of higher education and its diversity make it inhospitable to the kind of test-based accountability that NCLB has imposed on schools" ("Believe It"). He cautions us against this view and, as we will show throughout this book, his caution has become too well founded.

While no national requirement exists at this moment, an increasing number of institutions have implemented standardized tests anyway, often to answer increasing calls for accountability by cash-strapped states and by a public increasingly skeptical about the value of higher education. As the *New York Times* reported on April 7, 2012, an alliance of more than 300 colleges and universities, as well as organizations such as the Association for Public and Land-grant Universities and ACT, formed the Voluntary System of Accountability in response to the Spellings Commission report. This group both approves and encourages the use of the Educational Testing Service (ETS) Proficiency Profile, the ACT Collegiate Assessment of Academic Proficiency (CAAP) and the Collegiate Learning Assessment (CLA) (Perez-Peña). Further, the ongoing implementation of the Common Core State Standards (CCSS), their attendant tests, and the Core to College initiative represent some of the most well-funded systems of accountability we have ever seen. While the stated goal of the CCSS is to create a common set of milestones, or standards, for grades K–12, we will show how this effort is also working to change the educational landscape in our college classrooms, threatening our autonomy and diversity through a narrowing of articulation processes as well as our curricula in ways not unlike NCLB. However, we want to be clear that there is much within the CCSS that we applaud, it is how the standards are being funded and implemented, as well as how private testing companies are coopting and profiting from this effort, that causes great alarm.

We are especially concerned about what this might mean for writing instruction. Indeed, as Christopher Gallagher so clearly establishes,

> upper administrators, policy makers, and the general public continue to imagine faculty and students as targets of assessment rather than generators of it. In current educational discourse surrounding both K–12 and higher education, . . . assessment is envisioned primarily as a lever for institutional accountability and competition, rather than a teaching and learning practice. ("Being There" 452)

Similarly, Lil Brannon, in her 2011 CCCC's presentation, "Public Spaces, Private Interests: Teaching Writing in a Global Economy," traces the ways higher education is becoming increasingly privatized and, in the process, eroding the agency of faculty and students. This loss of agency is occurring as questions about curriculum and achievement are decided less and less by classroom-based educators and more and more by government entities, private testing companies, textbook companies, deep-pocketed think tanks, and private donors. The real danger, as Brannon argues, is that so very few of us even know what's going on. Perhaps this danger is nowhere more evident than in the implementation debates surrounding the Common Core State Standards. While forty-eight states initially signed onto the development and implementation of CCSS, a number of states have already rejected the standards or are considering doing so, offering reasons that vary from concerns about the developmental inappropriateness of the standards for young children to objections of a federal takeover of states' rights to determine the education of their citizens, to criticism of the ways the aligned standardized tests have been funded, designed, and implemented (Strauss).

In response to mounting criticism of CCSS, a group called Higher Ed for Higher Standards has formed. This is a project of the Collaborative for Student Success—a group that some view as little more than the public relations arm of the CCSS because the same groups that are designated as "backers" of CCSS are also backers of the Collaborative for Student Success and other CCSS outreach efforts. Higher Ed for Higher Standards has partnered with a long list of higher ed organizations representing hundreds of public and private schools including the American Association for Colleges and Universities, the Association of Public and Land-grant Universities, and the State Higher Education Executive Officers (SHEEO) associations. In addition, they count among their supporters prominent college and university presidents, chancellors, and other academic officers from every state (a full list can be found at http://highered forhigherstandards.org/supporters). In effect, just as criticism of CCSS reached a worrisome point, it looks like the higher education community has strongly positioned itself in support of CCSS, ready to defend these new standards as the best way to ensure college-ready students. But how many of us in higher education have read the Standards, let alone been given the opportunity to have a voice in defining the position of our institutions in relation to the Standards as well as their aligned standardized tests? And, for those of us in writing studies, how are the Common Core State Standards already shaping writing instruction in the United States—not just in K–12 classrooms, but in college classrooms as well?

This book offers a moment for all of us to take a look at the path higher education in general (and writing teachers and students in particular) are on, as calls for reform increasingly echo those of the later 1800s (a history we will discuss in Chapter One) and, more recently, those that led our nation to NCLB. We hope that this book will create opportunities to enter the national and local debates shaping writing studies, and embolden us to intervene in the current state of large-scale assessment primarily as a means of accountability and return it to a teaching and learning practice. It reminds us as teachers and researchers not to lose sight of the hard work of writing and writing instruction. We strive to understand what available data-driven research can and cannot tell us as we argue for a movement away from testing and accountability and toward best practices and standards at both the institutional and classroom level. We join Diane Ravitch, Christopher Gallagher, Lil Brannon, Kathleen Yancey, George Hillocks Jr., and others in their call to assert faculty and student agency in the form of leadership in the research and practice of writing instruction and assessment, as we all strive to reestablish the importance of writing in the twenty-first century.

§

In the chapters that follow, we untangle past, present, and emerging forces on the study and practice of writing at all levels of the curriculum. Included in this untangling is a report of our own large empirical study of writing instruction in a representative sample of U.S. secondary and post-secondary educational institutions. We provide historical and empirical grounding to support our call for teachers to pay greater attention to what is happening around us as well as to argue for the importance of genre, transfer, vertical curricula, empirical research and professional development, showing that these can help us meet the challenges and opportunities presented to writing teachers in the twenty-first century.

We begin in Chapter One with a historical exploration of calls for reform in writing instruction and assessment, going back to the 1800s, so that we can better understand the competing interests of our current moment. In particular, we examine calls for reform in writing instruction with a specific focus on how these calls have grown into demands for accountability as measured by standardized tests at all levels of the curriculum. Emphasis will be placed on the current state of the standardized testing movement at the college level, especially as it is shaped by the U.S. Department of Education's Report *A Test of Leadership: Charting the Future of U.S. Higher Education,* widely discussed critiques of writing in college such as that promoted in the popular book *Academically Adrift* (Arum and Roska), and recent reports on the use of standardized testing at the college level (e.g., a recently published report by the Council of Independent Colleges, "Catalyst for Change: The CIC/CLA Consortium"). In this chapter we will also touch on the probable effects the CCSS and their attendant standardized tests such as the PARCC assessment; their assessment was originally developed as a test of how well students in member states have mastered the CCSS, but is morphing into a college admissions test to rival the ACT and SAT, thus raising the stakes for standardized tests in our nation's high schools to a level not seen before. Chapter One paves the way for the rest of the book, which focuses on our analysis and response to calls for reform. We respond to calls for reform in four ways: (1) looking through an empirical lens at the actual practices of students and teachers through our own research, as well as a synthesis of multiple large-scale research projects; (2) scrutinizing the conflicts of interest and financially driven motives of private testing companies, deep-pocketed investors, and our own organizations such as the National Writing Project in the struggle for control over our educational systems; (3) highlighting curricular reforms that respond to the needs and values of learners, educators, policy makers and employers; and (4) providing examples of best practices at both the institutional and classroom level.

In Chapter Two, we report on our own empirical study of writing instruction in U.S. secondary and post-secondary education, systematically synthesizing the results of our study with the findings of recent survey and assessment research focused on the teaching and learning of writing. This will include large-scale studies such as the National Assessment of Educational Progress (NAEP), the National Survey of Student Engagement (NSSE), the National Commission on

Writing, institution-wide studies such as the Harvard Study of Writing, the Stanford Study of Writing, the Denver Longitudinal Study of Writing, and others, as well as our own research funded by the Conference on College Composition and Communication. In doing so, we offer a much needed corrective to the historical march outlined in Chapter One toward measuring the progress of our classrooms primarily through the lens of standardized tests at all levels of the curriculum. Instead, we offer a mixed-mode approach to articulating what is and isn't happening in writing classrooms. Our final goal in this chapter is to reveal patterns and relationships among the findings from various studies in order to argue for future directions in teaching and research.

While Chapter Two is rooted in a comparison of findings or results across studies concerning what does and doesn't work, Chapter Three is rooted in a comparison of conclusions or recommendations across studies based on these findings. Here we begin plotting a path forward, finding a surprising level of consensus about the path we should travel. We find the level of consensus surprising because of the wide-range of stakeholders involved, and because it varies significantly from the public rhetoric of accountability and testing so prevalent in our national discourse. At the same time, we begin to more fully integrate local and national discussions about the relatively new CCSS and how they are already influencing higher education in general (and writing studies in particular) into our overall argument. Indeed, the highly concerted efforts of the private and public entities backing the CCSS, as well as the unprecedented depth of their financial support, has already had a lasting effect and will continue to ensure that they and their aligned standardized tests have a significant place in our discussions for many years to come.

In Chapter Four, positioning ourselves as optimistic skeptics, we take a closer look at the potential role of CCSS in the future of writing instruction as we continue to scrutinize the conflicts of interest that permeate so much of the current state of educational reform. We also make a case for three very specific points of convergence that writing researchers and teachers in high school and college must pay attention to as we move forward, providing empirical evidence as well as tales from the field to argue for the value of forefronting these points of convergence. It is our belief that if we position ourselves as agents of change, aware of our potential roles as sponsors of literacy within the current historical moment, then we can effectively intervene in current efforts to shape writing instruction at the high school and college level. To do so, we argue for positioning ourselves at the confluence of Core to College initiatives, research on transfer emerging within rhetorical genre studies, and an investment in K–college professional learning communities at the local and national level. Based on the conclusions we reach in Chapters Three and Four, our final chapter, Chapter Five, argues that our ability to enact the policies and practices championed by our professional organizations rests on nothing less than a reassertion of the agency of students and teachers in the twenty-first century and beyond.

NOTE

1. Securing the participation of high schools was very difficult, in no small part due to the environment of surveillance and punishment, instead of exploration and inquiry, fostered by NCLB.

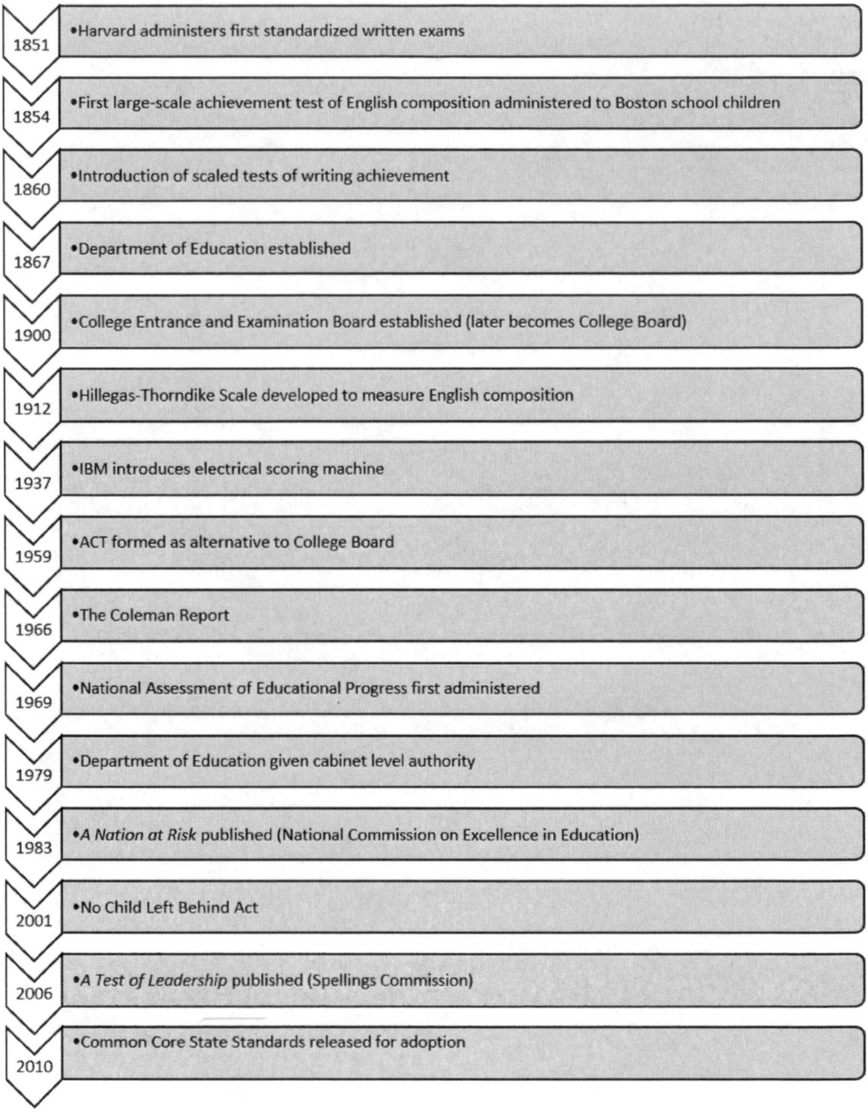

1851	•Harvard administers first standardized written exams
1854	•First large-scale achievement test of English composition administered to Boston school children
1860	•Introduction of scaled tests of writing achievement
1867	•Department of Education established
1900	•College Entrance and Examination Board established (later becomes College Board)
1912	•Hillegas-Thorndike Scale developed to measure English composition
1937	•IBM introduces electrical scoring machine
1959	•ACT formed as alternative to College Board
1966	•The Coleman Report
1969	•National Assessment of Educational Progress first administered
1979	•Department of Education given cabinet level authority
1983	•*A Nation at Risk* published (National Commission on Excellence in Education)
2001	•No Child Left Behind Act
2006	•*A Test of Leadership* published (Spellings Commission)
2010	•Common Core State Standards released for adoption

Figure 1.1. Timeline of Major Dates

CHAPTER 1

A BRIEF HISTORY OF ACCOUNTABILITY AND STANDARDIZED TESTING

In "Harvard, Again: Considering Articulation and Accreditation in Rhetoric and Composition's History," Ryan Skinnell demonstrates how the demand for articulation and its counterpart, accreditation, as larger institutional processes, have had profound effects on the development of writing instruction in the United States. He defines articulation as "the institutional protocol for connecting two or more types of schools (for example, secondary and post-secondary) so that students can move between them by virtue of well-defined processes" (96). In particular, he traces the impact of Harvard's need for improved articulation from high school to Harvard, and the resulting accreditation practices, as a significant shaping force on rhetoric and composition in the contemporary academy (49). Skinnell's work, in essence, positions these accreditation practices as an early example of the accountability measures increasingly at play in today's K–12 classrooms.

While Skinnell focuses narrowly on articulation and accreditation in relation to one particular institutional context, our investigation extends this view, looking at how calls for *accountability* contribute to the current rhetoric of crisis framing our national discourse on writing instruction. More specifically, we track how calls for accountability have increasingly resulted in the use of standardized tests of writing, despite little evidence that increased use of standardized testing over the last 150 years has led to improved writing or improved measurement of college readiness.

In fact, the most recent National Assessment of Educational Progress writing assessment reveals that only 24 percent of our eighth and twelfth graders performed at the proficient level, with just over half of them determined to perform at the basic level (partial mastery, not college-ready writers) (National Center for Educational Statistics 2012). This is despite many years of teachers laboring under the standardized testing requirements mandated by the No Child Left Behind Act. Further, George Hillocks Jr.'s extensive study of writing assessment in five states—Illinois, Kentucky, New York, Oregon, and Texas—"indicates that many writing assessments do not have the intended effects . . . [and] what they [teachers] are teaching appears to have a negative effect on the students in states with poorly thought out assessments" (205). In terms of standardized tests as a predictor of college readiness, we can point to a recent study released by the

National Association for College Admission Counseling—"Defining Promise: Optional Standardized Testing Policies in American College and University Admissions." This study asks whether or not standardized testing produces valuable predictive results, or if it limits the pool of applicants "who would succeed if they could be encouraged to apply" (Hiss and Frank 2). Examining data for 123,000 students at twenty private colleges and universities, six public universities, five minority-serving schools, and two arts schools, the researchers found that "the differences between submitters [of ACT or SAT scores] and non-submitters are five one-hundredths of a GPA point, and six-tenths of one percent in graduation rates. By any standard, these are trivial differences" (3). Equally important is the finding that those students who don't submit test scores are more likely to be first-generation, minorities, women, Pell Grant recipients, and students with learning differences (3).

Understanding the path that led to accountability through standardized testing is especially important for those of us working in higher education at this moment in time, as the use of standardized tests for students already in college (e.g., rising junior) increases every year.[1] Complicating matters further, two tests originally designed to measure student mastery of Common Core State Standards (CCSS),[2] PARCC (Partnership for Assessment of Readiness for College and Careers) and SBAC (Smarter Balanced Assessment Consortium), are also being adopted by some states for college placement and admissions.[3] For example, the Illinois State Board of Education's "PARCC Assessment FAQs" page states that "Institutions of higher education are working toward acceptance of PARCC assessment results as a way to show readiness for college-level work without remediation . . . allowing colleges and universities to place those students testing at the 'college and career ready' level in credit-bearing courses (as opposed to remedial courses)." The Colorado Department of Education's Communication Division Assessment Fact Sheet states online that "Colorado's new [2014] higher education admissions and remediation policies allow institutions to use PARCC scores for both course placement and admissions purposes."

As will become evident in this chapter, the recurring calls for educational reform that shape so much of our national discourse include standardized testing as one of the primary ways of enacting reform. These calls have more often than not resulted in increased use of standardized tests despite almost one hundred years of published debate and little consensus as to how well standardized testing can measure and improve educational performance. It is important to recognize that even though the results of standardized tests tell us very little about actual classroom practices, they have become the most visible and widely available measure of our classrooms. Finally, our exploration of calls for accountability through standardized testing strives to lay bare increasingly well-funded systems of control over our classrooms, as well as to deepen our understanding of emerging forces so that we can chart a path forward.

STANDARDIZED TESTING BEFORE SPUTNIK

While we often associate standardized testing of writing achievement with contemporary K–12 classrooms, standardized testing has long been commonplace in the United States. Most popular accounts identify the late 1960s as the beginning of *the* age of standardized testing, coming on the heels of America's perceived loss of the space race to Russia with the launch of Sputnik. For example, in 1969 Alice Rivlin, who is still considered one of America's leading economists, was asked to participate in a conference titled "The Measurement of Economic and Social Performance" (the proceedings of which were later published by the National Bureau of Economic Research). The planning of this conference coincided with the birth of the National Assessment of Educational Progress (NAEP), the first U.S. national test of academic achievement. Rivlin's task was to address the measurement of performance in education. She wrote:

> This is the age of testing. Considerable effort has gone into devising and standardizing a wide variety of tests of intellectual skills and accumulated knowledge. Billions of man-hours of student and teacher time are devoted to taking, administering, grading, analyzing, and discussing standardized tests. One might hope that all the effort would tell us something about output or performance in education.
>
> Remarkably, almost no information presently exists which would give a basis for constructing an index of change in educational test scores over time. (423)

We generally agree with Rivlin's characterization of the state of educational measurement at that time, but it is important to point out that standardized testing has a much longer and varied history than her paper and many accounts of the educational reform movement would make it seem. In fact, the late 1960s/early 1970s stand as just one of many periods during which standardized testing was a central measure of cultural and economic capital throughout history.

The 1860s mark the beginning of a visibly significant change in the history of U.S. universities as large numbers of students from disparate backgrounds began to seek a university education, defined academic disciplines became the organizing principle, and a professorate emerged that more closely resembles that of today. During this same time, Congress established the Department of Education (1867). Succumbing to intense pressure to keep the federal government out of what many saw as the province of the states, Congress demoted it to an Office of Education in 1868. The Office of Education spent time being shuffled between the Department of the Interior and the Federal Security Agency before settling in the Department of Health, Education, and Welfare. It was eventually given cabinet-level authority as the Department of Education in 1980 (U.S. Department of Education, *The Federal Role in Education*).

The main purpose of establishing the Department of Education in 1867 as described in the Act was to have an agency that gathered information on the condition and progress of our educational system:

> *Be it enacted by the Senate and House of Representatives of the*
> *United States of America in Congress assembled,* That there shall
> be established, at the city of Washington, a department of ed-
> ucation, for the purpose of collecting such statistics and facts
> as shall show the condition and progress of education in the
> several States and Territories, and of diffusing such informa-
> tion respecting the organization and management of schools
> and school systems, and methods of teaching, as shall aid the
> people of the United States in the establishment and main-
> tenance of efficient school systems, and otherwise promote
> the cause of education throughout the country. (An Act to
> establish a Department of Education, 1867)

Upon establishment of this department, a number of people began to advocate for the implementation of a national standardized exam. But a strong adherence to states' rights and logistical barriers to the implementation of a national exam kept such efforts at bay. In fact, it would be just over one hundred years after establishing a Federal Department of Education, in 1969, that the first national exam, the NAEP, was administered. Nonetheless, the mid-1800s and early 1900s marked a rapid expansion and development of educational testing and measurement in the United States—much of it through the efforts of our universities to influence curriculum at the secondary level in order to ensure students were prepared for university-level work. While these early efforts were not referred to in terms of accountability, but rather as a process of articulation, this process helped lay the groundwork for the systems of accountability at play today.

As early as 1833 Harvard and other colleges began to administer written exams as proof of achievement—the first in math (Black 192). By 1851, Harvard faculty recognized they could no longer assume students would arrive with a uniform set of skills, and in response instituted one of the first standardized, written entrance exams, focusing primarily on Latin grammar and math (Hanson 193) and, by the mid-1860s, including Greek composition, history, and geography. During this same time period, the number of children in government-funded schools began to swell, and public schools began to follow the example set by colleges in terms of measuring achievement. With increasing demand from universities for these schools to produce college-ready students, as well as the organization of boards of education in the states, standardized testing began to find solid footing in the United States.

The written standardized exam administered to all Boston school children in 1845 is thought to be the first large-scale achievement test of its kind, and a full account of this exam, including test questions, sample responses, and results, was collected for the 1925 edition of *Then and Now in Education, 1845:1923* (Caldwell and Courtis). Prior to 1845, the Boston public schools followed the standard practice of requiring oral exams administered by a traveling panel of examiners. But by 1845 there were 7,000 students in nineteen different schools, and this approach to measurement was no longer feasible. Instead, Boston instituted a written exam thought to be more objective, reliable, and economical than the oral exams (Mathison 3). The language sections of these tests focused on definitions and prescriptive grammar. Early examiners describe the condition and progress of education in Boston schools at this time in their report:

> The first feeling occasioned by looking over these returns is that of entire incredulity. It is very difficult to believe that, in the Boston Schools, there should be so many children in the first classes, unable to answer such questions; that there should be so many who try to answer, and answer imperfectly; that there should be so many absurd answers, so many errors in spelling, in grammar, and in punctuation. If by any accident these documents should be destroyed, we could hardly hope that your faith in our accuracy would induce you to believe the truth if we told it. But the papers are all before you, each signed by the scholar who wrote it. . . . The most striking results are shown in the attempts to give definitions to words. There were twenty-eight words selected from the reading book, which the classes have probably read through during the year, and some probably more than once. Some of these words are the very titles or headings of reading lessons; some of them occur several times in the book, and yet, of the 516 children who had these questions before them, one hour, not a single one defined correctly every word; only 47 defined half of them; and 29 could not define correctly a single one of the whole 28 words. (*Then and Now* 171, 175)

While most of these very early tests did not resemble those with which we are familiar today, it was not long before the basic structure of standardized tests of written communication were in place—a structure to which we still largely adhere. Standardization of writing tests took a significant leap forward in 1860 with the introduction of scaled tests of writing achievement. George Fisher, an English schoolteacher, provided us with the first written account of educators using anchor papers on a scale of 1–5 designed to measure writing achievement of large numbers of students. Fisher used these tests to assess handwriting, spelling, grammar, and composition (Bryant and Bryant 420). While it is not clear if the standard scale books themselves still exist, Fisher's description of them can be found in a copy of a paper he presented to the Statistical Section F, British Association, Cambridge, October 1, 1862:

On the Numerical Mode of Estimating and Recording Educational Qualifications As Pursued in the Greenwich Hospital Schools

It has been observed that "no mode of teaching can be properly appreciated so long as we are without recognized principles of examination, and accuracy in recording the results; for without such means neither failures nor improvements will add to our common stock of experience in such matters; and we hand down to posterity no statistical information of such value as will mark the progress of Education. . . .

Such a plan of numerical estimation has been carried out in the Greenwich Hospital Schools. A book, called the "Standard Scale-Book," has been there kept since the first general introduction of the plan containing the numerical value of each degree of proficiency in the various subjects of examination. If it be required, for instance, to determine the numerical equivalent to any specimen of writing, a comparison is made with various standard specimens of writing contained in this book, which are arrayed and numerically valued according to the degree of merit. The best executed being represented by the number 1, and the worst by the number 5. . . . So long as such standard specimens are preserved in the School, constant and permanent values for proficiency in writing can be maintained; and since facsimiles can now be multiplied with very little expense, it appears obvious that the same principle might be generally adopted, provided well-considered standards were agreed upon and recognized. . . .

I trust that I have made this mode of Registration as intel-
ligible to the Section as the present circumstances will admit
of. I have no other motive in making this communication to
them, beyond the desire of exciting the attention of others to
the subject, that it may lead to the adoption of some sound
practical system of testing and recording educational qualifi-
cations . . . according to some fixed standards of valuation as
might be generally agreed upon by those engaged in Education. (Excerpted from Cadenhead and Robinson 16–18)

Following Fisher's efforts to develop a standardized instrument to measure
writing achievement is the 1912 development of the Hillegas-Thorndike Scale
for the Measurement of Quality in English Composition by Young People. Dr.
Hillegas, a professor at Columbia University, believed that uniform standards
would establish a level of certainty when comparing the work of a student,
school, and system of schools with that of others. Further, if these measurements
of school performance: "approximate[ed] the accuracy of the scales used in measuring extension, weight, and time, educational administrators and investigators
would be able to measure and express the efficiency of a school system in terms
that would carry conviction" (2).

Development of the Hillegas-Thorndike Scale involved hundreds of people,
with final judgments resting in the hands of "28 individuals, nine of whom were
'men of special literary ability,' eleven 'gifted teachers familiar with secondary
education,' and eight 'psychologists familiar with the significance of scales and
zero points in the case of intellectual abilities and products'" (Johnson 40). Beginning with a sample of 7,000 essays divided into ten levels of ability, these
educational researchers developed a scale from 0–93 that eventually included
twenty-nine samples or anchor papers that were designed to allow for measurement of the "absolute gain which any pupil made in any year . . . the same
as his gain in height, weight, wages or pulse rate and the results of different
means and methods of teaching could be demonstrated with exactitude instead
of being guessed at" (Thorndike 214). We might consider this a very early type
of the "value-added assessments" that form the basis of many a "new" reform,
including pay-for-performance teacher contracts and the use of growth models.
Also interesting is that—whether rooted in a rubric or the use of model anchor papers (or both), whether based on evaluation by local teachers, experts,
or a software program, and whether on a small scale using performance-based
portfolios or a large scale using a spiraling, balanced incomplete design (e.g.,
NAEP)—scaled writing assessment is still the most common type of writing
assessment used at both local and national levels. In other words, when it comes

to assessing writing, we are still using a system originally developed in the 1860s in England and then later refined in the early 1900s in the United States.

The Hillegas-Thorndike Scale, and the goals of Hillegas and Thorndike themselves, were widely debated in composition teaching and research publications of the time, including numerous references from 1912–1925 in NCTE's *English Journal*. While many found the scale useful in very controlled contexts, most found it impractical due to the variation among genres, styles, grade levels, and other matters familiar to us today. As one critic pointed out, "You can not measure light, and warmth, and redness on the same rod" (Thomas 3) and, similarly, you can not measure all student writing achievement using the same rod (Thomas 3). Even in the twenty-first century, with technology unimagined in the early twentieth century, we are still using the same rod to measure student writing achievement. Rather than use technology to bring wide-scale innovation to this process, we have been content to focus on bringing economy of scale to the process.

One other major development requires mention in our brief history. In 1900, the College Entrance and Examination Board (CEEB) was established by a group of private high schools and elite colleges in order to standardize the admissions process and drive a more uniform curriculum at the private New England high schools from which the colleges drew most of their students. The CEEB later became College Board, a nonprofit testing agency most of us are familiar with as the administrator of the SAT. By the mid-1950s College Board was administering the Advanced Placement Program and soon developed the PSAT to measure students' critical reading and math skills in preparation for college entrance exams like the SAT and ACT. In 1959 ACT was formed as an alternative testing option to the SAT. Both of these organizations have grown immensely over the years, reaching ever farther into the educational landscape.

SPUTNIK: A MOMENT OF CRISIS

We've now returned to the point in our history where popular accounts of standardized testing and educational reform generally begin—Sputnik. Sputnik was the first artificial Earth satellite launched by the Soviet Union in 1957, signaling America's advertised loss of the space race. Homer Newell, a theoretical physicist and mathematician at the Naval Research Laboratory as well as NASA historian, recalls the moment:

> How brightly the Red Star shone before all the world in
> October of 1957! Streaking across the skies, steadily beeping
> its mysterious radio message to those on the ground, Sputnik
> was a source of amazement and wonder to people around

the globe, most of whom had had no inkling of what was about to happen. To one nation in particular the Russian star loomed as a threat and a challenge.

In the United States many were taken aback by the intensity of the reaction. Hysteria was the term used by some writers, although that was doubtless too strong a word. Concern and apprehension were better descriptions. Especially in the matter of possible military applications there was concern, and many judged it unthinkable that the United States should allow any other power to get into a position to deny America the benefits and protection that a space capability might afford. A strong and quick response was deemed essential. (Mudgway 75)

Many have and continue to use this event as proof of declining educational standards, particularly in math and science, making ample room for the argument that education is a matter of national security and the common good, and thus requires federal intervention. But Sputnik may be the most successful and persistent manufactured myth about the state of America's educational system to date. The crisis generated by this manufactured myth allowed for the political capital needed to pass the National Defense of Education Act[4] in 1958, opening the door to a national test of achievement—the NAEP—a giant leap toward the accountability movement that is now in full swing. Furthermore, this is a crisis that has remained a persuasive touchstone for educational reform movements for almost sixty years.

For example, Christopher Tienken and Donald Orlich remind us:

President Bill Clinton's Secretary of Education Richard Riley (1995) used Sputnik to justify further federal involvement in education as part of the America 2000 legislation: "When the Russians woke us up by flying Sputnik over our heads late at night—a few of you may remember that experience—Congress passed the 1958 National Defense of Education Act, which sent millions of Americans to college and educated a generation of scientists who helped us to win the Cold War." Ronald Reagan used Sputnik as a propaganda tool in 1982 to support his plan to give tax credits for parents to send their students to private schools. (25)

And in his 2011 State of the Union Address, President Obama declared: "This is our generation's Sputnik moment. . . . But if we want to win the future—if we want innovation to produce jobs in America and not overseas—then we also have to win the race to educate our kids. That's why instead of just pouring money into a system that's not working, we launched a competition called Race to the Top."

But Tienken and Orlich assert that recently declassified documents from the Eisenhower administration "tell another story of Sputnik. Sputnik became a manufactured crisis, to borrow a term by Berliner and Biddle" (21). It's important to keep in mind that, at this time, the federal government had very little to do with our K–12 curriculum, and attempts by the federal government to shape curriculum were easily rebuked. Sputnik was quickly framed as tangible, startling evidence of a broken educational system, and a crisis of opportunity ensued. But there is significant evidence showing that the launch of Sputnik had nothing to do with the state of our educational system. For example, a memorandum of conference with President Eisenhower on October 8, 1957, quotes then Deputy Secretary of Defense Quarles, as saying, "the Redstone [military rocket] had it been used could have orbited a satellite a year or more ago" (qtd. in Tienken and Orlich 21).

NASA's own history of Charles Pickering, director of the Jet Propulsion Laboratory from 1954 to 1976, also tells a story of Sputnik much different than that continually forwarded by our leaders when arguing for school reform efforts. Pickering's own account of the nation's reaction to Sputnik reveals the sense of helplessness and urgency this event elicited:

> The reaction in this country was amazing. People were startled to realize that this darn thing was going overhead about ten times per day and there was not a thing they could do about it—and realizing that what was thought to be a nation of peasants could do something like this—with this amount of technical complexity. (qtd. in Mudgway 75).

Pickering and his staff at the Jet Propulsion Laboratory not only knew how to launch a satellite into space, they had all the hardware they needed in order to do it. "All they lacked was the approval to 'go ahead.' . . . But the word to 'go ahead' did not come" (Mudgway 75). It is beyond the scope of this book to explore the reasons why the United States held off on its launch of a satellite—many of which center on concerns about the state of the Cold War at the time. Of importance to our discussion, one of the unexpected results of the decision to delay the launch was the passage of the National Defense of Education Act, the first federal policy to largely target higher education while also directing funds to improving instruction in math, science, and modern foreign languages (e.g., Russian) in our K–12 classrooms.

THE PRODUCT OF AN EXTENSIVE SURVEY REQUESTED BY THE CIVIL RIGHTS ACT OF 1964, THIS REPORT DOCUMENTS THE AVAILABILITY OF EQUAL EDUCATIONAL OPPORTUNITIES IN THE PUBLIC SCHOOLS FOR MINORITY GROUP NEGROES, PUERTO RICANS, MEXICAN-AMERICANS, ORIENTAL-AMERICANS, AND AMERICAN INDIANS, AS COMPARED WITH OPPORTUNITIES FOR MAJORITY GROUP WHITES. COMPARATIVE ESTIMATES ARE MADE ON A REGIONAL AS WELL AS ON A NATIONAL BASIS. SPECIFICALLY, THE REPORT DETAILS THE DEGREE OF SEGREGATION OF MINORITY GROUP PUPILS AND TEACHERS IN THE SCHOOLS AND THE RELATIONSHIP BETWEEN STUDENTS' ACHIEVEMENT, AS MEASURED BY ACHIEVEMENT TESTS, AND THE KINDS OF SCHOOLS THEY ATTEND. EDUCATIONAL QUALITY IS ASSESSED IN TERMS OF CURRICULUMS OFFERED, SCHOOL FACILITIES SUCH AS TEXTBOOKS, LABORATORIES, AND LIBRARIES, SUCH ACADEMIC PRACTICES AS TESTING FOR APTITUDE AND ACHIEVEMENT, AND THE PERSONAL, SOCIAL, AND ACADEMIC CHARACTERISTICS OF THE TEACHERS AND THE STUDENT BODIES IN THE SCHOOLS. ALSO IN THE REPORT IS A DISCUSSION OF FUTURE TEACHERS OF MINORITY GROUP CHILDREN, CASE STUDIES OF SCHOOL INTEGRATION, AND SECTIONS ON HIGHER EDUCATION OF MINORITIES AND SCHOOL NONENROLLMENT RATES. INFORMATION RELEVANT TO THE SURVEY'S RESEARCH PROCEDURES IS APPENDED. NOTABLE AMONG THE FINDINGS ON THE SURVEY ARE THAT NEGRO STUDENTS AND TEACHERS ARE LARGELY AND UNEQUALLY SEGREGATED FROM THEIR WHITE COUNTERPARTS, AND THAT THE AVERAGE MINORITY PUPIL ACHIEVES LESS AND IS MORE AFFECTED BY THE QUALITY OF HIS SCHOOL THAN THE AVERAGE WHITE PUPIL. THIS DOCUMENT IS ALSO AVAILABLE FROM THE SUPERINTENDENT OF DOCUMENTS, U.S. GOVERNMENT PRINTING OFFICE, WASHINGTON, D.C. 20402, FOR $4.25. (AH)

Figure 1.1 Abstract from Coleman Report

But it wasn't just the perceived loss of the space race that finally led to a national exam. *Equality of Educational Opportunity for All,* often referred to as the Coleman Report, may have had an equally important effect. The Coleman Report was commissioned by the U.S. Office of Education and published in 1966. It "marks the first time there is made available a comprehensive collection of data gathered on consistent specifications throughout the whole nation" (Coleman 1). Approximately 645,000 students from 4,000 public schools in grades 3, 6, 9, and 12 participated in this research, which focused on the extent to which equality of education was a reality for America's school children.

This was a landmark study leading to a flurry of activity but, as many argue, little in the way of educational progress. As a brief aside, we can link The Colman Report with claims such as those of Berliner that the real education crisis is a crisis of poverty, not a crisis of overall educational achievement. In a retrospective on The Coleman Report, Adam Gorman and Daniel Long of the Wisconsin Center for Education Research found that forty years later the major findings of the report hold up well, most notably that per-pupil spending is less important than level of teacher training, the black-white achievement gap persists, and "Student achievement still varies substantially within schools . . . and this variation is still tied to students' social and economic backgrounds" (19). In fact, when discussing the 2015 reauthorization of the Elementary and Secondary Education Act, Secretary of Education Arne Duncan prioritized equity for low-income and minority students because "Education Department data show that 6.6 million students from low-income families are being shortchanged when it comes to state and local education funding" (U.S. Department of Education, "Secretary Duncan"). For example, the education department estimates that in Pennsylvania, the highest-poverty districts spend 33 percent less than the lowest-poverty districts, while in Vermont, Illinois, Missouri, and Virginia, the highest-poverty districts spend 18–17 percent less than the lowest-poverty districts. And in Nevada, the highest-minority districts spend 30 percent less than the lowest-minority districts, while in Nebraska and Arizona, the highest-minority districts spend 17–15 percent less than the lowest-minority districts (U.S. Department of Education, "Secretary Duncan").

Importantly, it is difficult to attract, retain, and develop high-quality teachers in high-poverty schools (Clotfelter, Ladd, and Vigdor 2005; Grissom 2011). A 2014 report by the Alliance for Excellent Education estimates that 13 percent of our teachers move or leave the teaching profession each year: "This high turnover rate disproportionately affects high-poverty schools and seriously compromises the nation's capacity to ensure that all students have access to skilled teaching" (Haynes). This is especially problematic when we consider that, as Ben Ost says, "one of the most consistent findings in the literature on teacher quality is that teachers improve with experience" (1).

Most studies of teacher turnover in high-poverty schools have attributed turnover to characteristics of the students and the teachers, rather than the organizational structure of the schools themselves—organizational structures that can be improved with increased funding. Emerging research on teacher turnover in high-poverty schools suggests "when these teachers leave, it is frequently because the working conditions in their schools impede their chance to teach and their students' chance to learn" (Simon and Johnson 4). Organizational factors that are associated with higher rates of turnover include administrative support, teacher input in decision-making, salary, and aspects of school culture (Simon and Johnson 12). We will return to a discussion of some of these factors in our last chapter, but for the moment let's turn back to our history of standardized testing.

The ability tests collected as part of The Coleman Report were administered by ETS and the language section focused on items such as sentence completion and identifying analogies—items that could easily and efficiently be measured. This is not surprising given the number of students involved in this study and research appearing as early as the 1940s claiming a high correlation between objective tests (tests of grammar, spelling, punctuation, and capitalization) and final grades in rhetoric courses. For example, Irwin A. Berg, Graham Johnson, and Robert P. Larsen detail a study conducted in 1943 wherein the researchers agree that under ideal conditions writing proficiency can only be determined by a demonstration of writing, but also argue that an objective test is correlated highly enough with final grades in rhetoric courses that "the advantages of rapid scoring which could be done by persons who are not necessarily rhetoric instructors, together with the advantages of objectivity of score, would make the use of a suitable objective test an extremely practical measuring tool" (430). Of further note, the objective test used in this study was scored by an International Business Machines electrical scoring machine, a machine first introduced in 1937 that allowed for scoring of large numbers of standardized tests on a new scale. Much like the history of standardized tests of writing instruction, arguments for the use of machine-graded scoring to assess writing ability have a much longer history than many of our current discussions reveal. And, it is these histories that we must begin to more fully understand if we are to reassert the agency of teachers and students in the current clash over the control of literacy.

While The Coleman Report was intended as a massive, one-time educational measurement and analysis effort, the NAEP writing assessment, also known as *The Nation's Report Card*, was intended to be repeated on a regular basis, allowing for comparison of educational progress over time. The NAEP tests students in different subjects each year, with a writing test first administered in 1969/70 and repeated approximately every four years. The overarching goal of NAEP, as stated in the 1969/70 writing report, is to assess educational attainment on a national basis; it is also to offer "descriptions of what groups of Americans know and can do and, over a period of time, of whether there is progress in educational attainments" (1). Finally, Americans would know how our students are performing not just during any given year, but also over time, so that we could track educational progress. While this plan has worked relatively well for reading and math, the same two subjects mandated for yearly assessment by NCLB, it has not worked for writing. Instead, teachers and administrators who have looked at the results of such tests for guidance are often left confounded. An account written in 1992 by Mary Licklider, a junior high English teacher, is representative:

> The Nation's Report Card on Writing issued by the National
> Assessment of Educational Progress (NAEP) in June 1990 left
> me frustrated and confused. I could not tell whether students'
> writing had declined or improved since 1970. From the tone
> of the report I suspected the former. As an English teacher, I
> thought I might be more effective selling shoes . . . Surely, the

> extensive resources of NAEP, including a massive data bank
> covering two decades, might yield information that teachers
> need if they are to become better teachers of writing. I feel
> somewhat short changed by the reports I have read; and I
> have been unable to obtain essential NAEP documents even
> with the help of interlibrary loan operating through our local
> public library and reaching out of state as well. (34, 39)

In fact, NAEP did attempt to produce long-term trend reports for writing, but by 1999 had abandoned this effort, explaining that the content and manner of administration had changed so much from test to test that the accuracy of the results were called into question (Phillips). Curiously, while it is possible to track down these reports via used bookstores and microfiche, they can no longer be easily accessed online via the Education Resources Information Center (ERIC) or the NAEP website.

The problem of large-scale writing assessment is stated very clearly by Arthur Applebee, drawing on a paper he was commissioned to write by the National Assessment Governing Board (overseers of the NAEP since 1988) in 2005 as they worked to develop a framework for the 2011 NAEP writing assessment:

> Underlying all of the specific issues that follow is a larger
> one: What information about how students write should
> NAEP and other large-scale assessments provide to interested
> members of the general public, policymakers, and educators?
> Although it is a seemingly simple question, buried within it
> are a variety of difficult issues on which there is currently little
> consensus, including how to describe the domain of writing
> tasks; the relationships among component skills, content
> knowledge, and generalized writing "fluency"; and the rele-
> vance of computer-based applications to definitions of writing
> achievement as well as to assessment techniques. ("Issues" 82)

In other words, writing is an extremely complex and ever-changing human activity, continually influenced by evolving cultural norms and technological advancements. Pinning it down for large-scale assessment over time simply hasn't been possible. If an examination of long-term trends using the only large-scale, longitudinal studies publicly available teaches us anything, it is how exceedingly difficult it is to measure the writing achievement of students in rigorous and valid ways over any extended period of time using a single measurement tool such as a standardized test—especially in ways that can guide instruction. This is not to say that a national assessment of writing instruction isn't useful, but rather that a test has yet to be developed that can reliably measure change in writing achievement over time due to the rapidly changing writing demands placed on students and workers.

Despite the misgivings of the National Assessment Governing Board itself, and constant revision and critique of attempts to assess writing over time, many were not deterred by these concerns and instead began to argue for the use of such tests within higher education.

STANDARDIZED TESTING AND HIGHER EDUCATION

We began this chapter with a section from Alice Rivlin's presentation at the Measurement of Social and Economic Performance Conference in 1969. After arguing that most aspects of educational performance can and should be measured, Rivlin concludes:

> Test scores and other performance measures are now being used as evidence against educators. It seems likely that educators will respond by developing more comprehensive and reliable measures of their own, not only to satisfy the public, but to put their own house in order and build into the management of education some measures of what is being produced and some incentives to produce it more effectively. (427–28)

Within higher education, it is the case that many educators and the professional organizations that represent them responded by developing comprehensive and reliable measures of their own. For example, the National Institute for Learning Outcomes Assessment, established in 2008 and located in the School of Education at the University of Illinois at Urbana-Champaign, holds as its mission to "discover and disseminate ways that academic programs and institutions can productively use assessment data internally to inform and strengthen undergraduate education, and externally to communicate with policy makers, families and other stakeholders."[5] The multidimensional toolkit they propose includes tests, surveys, portfolios, curriculum mapping, benchmarking, handbooks, and rubrics.

As another example, the Peer Review of Teaching Project (PRTP), begun in 1994 and currently housed at the University of Nebraska-Lincoln

> is a faculty-driven approach for developing a campus climate for teaching improvement and reform. Invited faculty work in teams over the course of a year to discuss approaches for documenting and assessing student learning within particular

courses. Rather than advocating any particular teaching approach or technique, the PRTP focuses on helping faculty document student learning occurring in their course and then reflect on whether student performance demonstrates achievement of the curricular and department goals.[6]

Specifically in relation to writing classrooms, we might look to the National Council of Teachers of English and the Council of Writing Program Administrators' (NCTE-WPA) "White Paper on Writing Assessment in Colleges and Universities, the Conference on College Composition and Communication's (CCCC) "Writing Assessment Principles," the collaboration between WPA and the National Survey of Student Engagement, and the Valid Assessment of Learning in Undergraduate Education (VALUE) Rubric for Written Communication offered by the Association of American Colleges and Universities through their VALUE Rubric Development Project. All of these efforts propose pedagogically sound, empirically based assessment practices. However, for multiple reasons, these efforts have not satisfied the public or deterred calls for more standardized testing and accountability. Instead, we have found ourselves in a defensive position, as evidenced by the establishment of the NCTE Rapid Response Assessment Task Force in 2014. Led by Kathleen Yancey, this task force was created "to address the growing cacophony around assessment" from a very activist stance.

In the remainder of this chapter, we will look at two defining texts and one potentially major shift in public policy agenda setting in the call for more standardized testing at the college level that epitomize the need for work such as that of the NCTE Rapid Response Assessment Task Force. The two texts are *A Test of Leadership: Charting the Future of U.S. Higher Education* (a report of the commission appointed by Secretary of Education Margaret Spellings, also known as the Spellings Report) and one of the most widely discussed books calling for reform of higher education, *Academically Adrift* (Arum and Roksa). Examining these texts within the context of their history increases our understanding of present and emerging forces so that we can chart a path forward. We will conclude with an exploration of the shift toward advocacy philanthropy and the emerging role of foundations in directing policy and practices in U.S. higher education.

As explained in our introduction, our current work is motivated by many happenings in 2006, including efforts to set higher education on the same path as K–12 through the No Child Left Behind Act. It is the 2006 report commissioned by then Secretary of Education Margaret Spellings that aimed to establish systems of accountability, punishment, and reward not seen before in higher education. Echoing the same threats to the American Dream and the Common

Good as its predecessors, the National Defense of Education Act and *A Nation at Risk*, the U.S. Department of Education's *A Test of Leadership: Charting the Future of U.S. Higher Education* urges a "robust culture of accountability" (20):

> We believe that improved accountability is vital to ensuring the success of all the other reforms we propose. Colleges and universities must become more transparent about cost, price, and student success outcomes, and must willingly share this information with students and families. Student achievement, which is inextricably connected to institutional success, must be measured by institutions on a "value-added" basis that takes into account students' academic baseline when assessing their results. This information should be made available to students, and reported publicly in aggregate form to provide consumers and policymakers an accessible, understandable way to measure the relative effectiveness of different colleges and universities. (4)

Interestingly, and very much in line with the rhetoric and practice of No Child Left Behind, the authors of this report note in their introductory summary that, "According to the most recent National Assessment of Adult Literacy . . . the percentage of college graduates deemed proficient in prose literacy has actually declined from 40 to 31 percent in the past decade" (3). And yet, in its recommendations, the commission "urge[s] these institutions to develop new pedagogies, curricula and technologies to improve learning, *particularly in the areas of science and mathematics*" (5, emphasis ours), choosing not to place an emphasis on writing in U.S. schools.

A Test of Leadership names specific standardized tests, such as the Collegiate Learning Assessment (CLA), for use in our colleges as a means of rigorous accountability. The CLA was developed under the auspices of the Council for Aid to Education (CAE), a nonprofit organization initially established in 1952 to encourage corporate support of education. The CAE currently conducts policy research on higher education as well as focuses on improving quality and access in higher education, primarily through the CLA, and now CLA+ (a revision of CLA). CAE describes CLA+ as a way for national and international institutions to "benchmark value-added growth in student learning at their college or institution compared to other institutions." CAE uses "performance-based tasks . . . to evaluate the critical-thinking and written-communication skills of college students. It measures analysis and problem solving, scientific and quantitative reasoning, critical reading and evaluation, and critiquing argument, in addition to writing mechanics and effectiveness" ("CLA+ Overview"). Our primary concern here is not with the CLA itself. Although we do find some of the claims about the use and value of CLA to be problematic, as we explain later, within clearly defined and well-understood parameters it can be a useful tool, although only when combined with other measures of educational progress.

Instead, our primary concern with the CLA is the way that it is employed in the name of accountability, following the example of one of the most popular books on higher education today—*Academically Adrift*—which has been touted by those on the right, left, and center as proof of a failing system of higher education in need of unprecedented levels of control and accountability. As noted by many researchers, it took just over a year for the central touchstone of this book, that 45 percent of the students in the study failed to show significant gains in reasoning and writing skills between the beginning of their freshman year and the end of their sophomore year, to establish itself as central tenet of U.S. folklore about higher education (see, e.g., Astin, Lane and Oswald). Like many others, we have great concerns about the statistical analysis in *Academically Adrift* and its sweeping claims based on a study of only slightly more than 2,300 college students. But perhaps more importantly, from our perspective as writing researchers, we have serious concerns about the claims made by CLA that it is testing "general" reasoning and writing skills and, furthermore, that the results of a 90-minute performance-based task can measure the writing abilities of students over time.

The authors of *Academically Adrift*, with the help of CLA, enlisted twenty-four colleges of varying sizes and classifications to participate in their research. It is important to note that they do not include community college students in their research sample, and further, of the 2,300 students who volunteered to participate in this study, very few were considered to be of low scholastic ability. This is important because community college students and students of lower scholastic ability are likely to exhibit the most growth during their college career. Further, this book focuses on the results of just one performance task, giving students "ninety minutes to respond to a writing prompt that is associated with a set of background documents" (21).

The details of the statistical errors made by the authors have been explained by many researchers. For example, the authors set the level of statistical significance at .05—a relatively arbitrary starting point. Using this number, they claim that 45 percent of the students in this study did not improve their reasoning and writing skills because the overall change in scores was not statistically significant. As Alexander Astin points out in the *Chronicle of Higher Education*, "Just because the amount of improvement in a student's CLA score is not large enough to be declared 'statistically significant' does not prove that the student failed to improve his or her reasoning and writing skills" (4). In fact, as Richard Haswell makes clear, "every one of their twenty-seven subgroups recorded gain" (488), but the authors of *Academically Adrift* claim that this gain was "modest" or "limited" based on their set standard of statistical significance. Equally concerning, as Haswell explains, "Not one piece of past research showing undergraduate improvement in writing and critical thinking—and there are hundreds—appears in the authors' discussion or their bibliography, although both are a swim with think-tank books and blue-ribbon papers opining the opposite" (488).

Examined from another angle, Lane and Oswald make the case that:

> This 45% finding is, indeed, shocking—but for a completely different reason. Considering that each significance test was based on a sample size of 1 (i.e., each student's change in the CLA measure), it is hard to imagine that as many as 55 percent of students would show statistically significant gains. Indeed, one would expect to find an order of magnitude fewer significant improvements, based on the mean difference between the pre- and post-tests the authors reported in their study. The reason Arum and Roska found that so many (not so few) students improved significantly is that they computed the wrong significance test.

This particular problem is further highlighted in a paper published by the CLA itself titled *The Collegiate Learning Assessment: Facts and Fantasies*, in which they make clear that "The CLA focuses on the institution (rather than the student) as the unit of analysis . . . [and] The CLA itself does not identify the reasons why a school's students do better or worse than expected" (Klein, et al. 3).

But for those of us not statistically inclined, there are other glaring problems with claims that this standardized test of writing can be used to measure change in student ability over time. In fact, these problems seem to echo the very same ones that caused the National Assessment of Educational Progress to question the validity and reliability of their long-term trend assessments in writing and, ultimately, to declare them not reliable or valid enough upon which to make claims about change in writing achievement over time. The first problem is whether or not the writing tasks and the measurement tools used at two different intervals were controlled to a level that would allow for valid and reliable comparison of change over time. It is important to emphasize that they *seem* to echo these problems because the authors of *Academically Adrift* will not release the actual pre- and post-writing prompts used in their research so that those who specialize in writing assessment and test development can measure the validity and reliability of their claims. This unwillingness to engage in full peer review, especially to a degree that would allow others to determine the validity and re-liability of their results through means such as replicability, certainly calls their research and motives into question.

The second problem concerns the writing tasks themselves. CLA and the authors of *Academically Adrift* emphasize numerous times that their perfor-mance-based assessments of writing are authentic and based on *general skills* as opposed to *specific content knowledge* gained through exposure to the primary texts in one's major or discipline. They point to the following performance-based assessment as representative of a task requiring only *general skills*:

> The "DynaTech" performance task asks students to generate a memo advising an employer about the desirability of purchas-ing a type of airplane that has recently crashed. Students are informed: "You are the assistant to Pat Williams, the president of DynaTech, a company that makes precision electronic instruments and navigational equipment. Sally Evans, a mem-ber of DynaTech's sales force, recommended that DynaTech buy a small private plane (a SwiftAir 235) that she and other members of the sales force could use to visit customers. Pat was about to approve the purchase when there was an acci-dent involving a SwiftAir 235." Students are provided with the following set of documents for this activity: newspaper articles about the accident, a federal accident report on in-flight breakups in single engine planes, Pat Williams' e-mail to her assistant and Sally Evans' e-mail to Pat Williams, charts on SwiftAir's performance characteristics, an article from *Am-ateur Pilot* magazine comparing the SwiftAir 235 to similar planes, and pictures and descriptions of SwiftAir models 180 and 235. Students are then instructed to "prepare a memo that addresses several questions, including what data support or refute the claim that the type of wing on the SwiftAir 235 leads to more in-flight breakups, what other factors might have contributed to the accident and should be taken in account, and your overall recommendation about whether or not DynaTech should purchase the plane. (*Academically Adrift*, 21–22)

Of course, there is the obvious problem of the timed nature of this task, as no one of any repute would tackle such a serious writing task in ninety min-utes. Perhaps more perplexing is that it is difficult at best to understand how a prompt requiring knowledge of a discipline-specific genre, a formal business memo, about a discipline-specific subject, aerospace engineering, within the context of another specific field, risk management, could be considered a test of general knowledge. Further, this is an "authentic" test for a very, very small subset of our society—those in the position to make high-level risk management decisions. Again, it is troubling that neither the authors of *Academically Adrift* nor CLA will release the actual performance prompts used. But, if the above performance prompt is representative, as the authors claim, then it is very likely that students were not tested on general knowledge but rather very genre- and discipline-specific knowledge and, further that the genres and disciplines were different in the pre- and post-tests. Nonetheless, this ill-conceived study continues to be used as one of the primary arguments for enacting greater systems of accountability in higher education writing classrooms.

DIRECTING FUTURE ATTENTION

Margaret Strain concludes in her article "In Defense of a Nation: The National Defense of Education Act, Project English, and the Origins of Empirical Research in Composition": "By seeing historical events as a dynamic interplay of resistance and persuasion among groups of varied power, we are able to recognize and appreciate the competing interests that inform a historical moment" (533). We would add that this type of work also allows us to chart a path forward as emerging entanglements in the struggle to control literacy are revealed. As we bring this phase of our investigation to a close, we move toward understanding how all of this may reshape composition classrooms. Specifically, we are concerned about the possible effects of the Common Core State Standards, not in and of themselves, but in and of their relationship to standardized tests of writing on the field of rhetoric and composition. The CCSS are self-described as:

> a set of high-quality academic standards in mathematics and English language arts/literacy (ELA). These learning goals outline what a student should know and be able to do at the end of each grade. The standards were created to ensure that all students graduate from high school with the skills and knowledge necessary to succeed in college, career, and life, regardless of where they live. Forty-four states, the District of Columbia, four territories, and the Department of Defense Education Activity (DoDEA) have voluntarily adopted and are moving forward with the Common Core.[7]

Much like the earlier rhetoric of crisis following Sputnik that led to the National Assessment of Educational Progress and was echoed in *A Test of Leadership* and its attendant calls for systems of accountability, the CCSS are being propelled by a fear that the United States is falling dangerously behind other countries in global tests of academic achievement. As the October 7, 2013, issue of *Time* proclaimed: "What's driving the core standards conversation now is the ambition to succeed in a global economy and the anxiety that American students are failing to do so" (Meacham 44). This crisis rhetoric can be found in the Council on Foreign Relations Task Force's report *US Education Reform and National Security* that argues a failing U.S. education system threatens our national security in five specific ways: "threats to economic growth and competitiveness, U.S. physical safety, intellectual property, U.S. global awareness, and U.S. unity and cohesion" (qtd. in Klein and Rice 7). Further, while critiques of the CCSS abound, overall their adoption has been swift and ongoing as textbooks are realigned, tests developed, school district rubrics restructured, and teachers trained. In fact, as mentioned in our introduction, when a small number of governors began to publicly denounce CCSS after previously adopting the standards, the group Higher Ed for Higher Standards was formed and includes over 200 presidents, chancellors, state officials, and organizations such as the American Association of Colleges and Universities (AAC&U). Much like Harvard in the 1800s, this group is working to establish processes of articulation, this time via CCSS. Perhaps not surprisingly, this coalition is part of the Collaborative for Student Success, funded in large part by the Bill and Melinda Gates Foundation (Mangan), the primary investor in the CCSS itself.

The conflicts of interest in terms of how the CCSS are being funded and implemented forebode systems of accountability and measurement that will rest heavily on writing instruction at the college level. Thomas Newkirk begins to unravel these conflicts in "Speaking Back to the Common Core":

> The Common Core State Standards are joined at the hip to standardized tests, not surprising because both the College Board and the ACT have had such a big role in their creation. It was clear from their conception that they would play a large part in teaching evaluation, a requirement for applications for Race to the Top funds and exemptions from No Child Left Behind. (4)

For example, David Coleman, who became the president of College Board in 2012, and thus overseer of the SAT, is not only one of the major initiators of the CCSS, but one of the people who convinced Bill and Melinda Gates to fund them. Bill Gates did more than simply fund their development; he "was de facto organizer, providing money and structure for states to work together on common standards in a way that avoided the usual collision between states' rights and national interests that had undercut every previous effort" (Layton). Coleman went on to write much of the standards for math and literacy. Most recently, in many well-publicized events, he announced that the SAT will be re-designed to align with the CCSS. One of the changes includes making the essay part of the exam optional. The entanglements don't end here. As reported in the November 3, 2013, issue of the *Chronicle of Higher Education*, the Bill and Melinda Gates Foundation hired Richard Arum, one of the authors of *Academically Adrift*, as a senior fellow on educational quality.

The influence of private foundations reaches far beyond investment in the development of the standards. For example, the National Writing Project is now significantly funded in part by the Bill and Melinda Gates Foundation, and this funding reaches down into local sites specifically in an increased effort to gain compliance with the CCSS. In 2010 The National Writing Project received a $550,000 grant from the Bill & Melinda Gates Foundation and teams of teachers were expected to "create a model for classroom teachers in writing instruction across the curriculum that will support students to achieve the outcomes of the Common Core Standards" ("To Create"). In 2011 the Bill and Melinda Gates Foundation awarded $3,095,593 in grant money to local sites of the National Writing Project to "create curricula models for classroom teachers in writing instruction that will support students to achieve the outcomes of the newly state-adopted Common Core Standards" ("Denver Writing Project"). In 2014, the Bill and Melinda Gates Foundation funded the Assignments Matter program. These grants were designed to "introduce large numbers of teachers to the Literacy Design Collaborative (LDC) and its tools for making and sharing writing assignments. Specifically, we will introduce teachers to the LDC task bank and jurying rubric, tools meant to support teachers in creating clear and meaningful writing prompts" ("Assignments Matter").

While the official website for the Common Core State Standards emphasizes the flexibility teachers have in developing curriculum, the Literacy Design Collaborative belies what may appear to be support for teacher agency. In 2013, the Bill and Melinda Gates Foundation directed $12,000,000 to "incubate an anchor Literacy Design Collaborative (LDC) organization to further expand reach and impact [of the Common Core State Standards]" (Literacy Design Collaborative, Inc.). On their official website, the LDC purports to put "educators in the lead" but only in so much as they operate within the relatively narrow parameters of rubrics designed and approved by the Collaborative. For example:

> [LDC] has created a process to validate the CCRS align-
> ment of LDC-created content. The SCALE-created "jurying"
> process looks at how richly the tasks and modules engage

> academic content and build CCRS-aligned skills. Jurying can
> provide guidance on how to improve each module and is used
> to identify modules that are ready to share, as well as to spot-
> light those that reach the standards for "exemplary" that are in
> the LDC Curriculum Library. ("Overview")

Furthermore, teachers are expected to use the LDC developed rubrics when assessing student work:

> After a module's instructional plan is taught and students'
> final products (their responses to the teaching task) are
> collected, teachers score the work using LDC rubrics that
> are focused on key CCRS-aligned features as well as on the
> disciplinary knowledge shown in each piece. Visit the Ru-
> bric page for more information. ("Overview")

The LDC claims to have "enabled" tens of thousands of teachers to prepare students for the 21st Century workforce. With a $12,000,000 initial investment by the Bill and Melinda Gates Foundation, the LDC has the resources needed to incentivize and build professional development activities that are highly regulated and closely aligned with CCSS.

Perhaps of more direct importance to the field of rhetoric and composition is the Core to College initiative. Core to College is a sponsored project of Rockefeller Philanthropy Advisors and is funded by the Lumina Foundation, the William and Flora Hewlett Foundation, the Bill and Melinda Gates Foundation, and the Carnegie Corporation of New York. According to the Rockefeller Philanthropy Advisors, eleven states—Colorado, Florida, Hawaii, Indiana, Kentucky, Louisiana, Massachusetts, North Carolina, Oregon, Tennessee and Washington—have been provided with funds to use the CCSS to drive curricular alignment in academic courses and sequences, data and accountability, and teacher development (Rockefeller). Each of these twelve states has an Alignment Director (AD) whose job is to oversee the Core to College initiative in his or her state. WestEd has been retained to track progress of this initiative. In 2013, WestEd released their report "Implementing the Common Core State Standards: Articulating Course Sequences Across K–12 and Higher Education Systems" (Finkelstein, et. al). Interestingly, even though the primary goal of this initiative is to align course sequencing and instruction across K–12 and higher education systems, and even though there is widespread belief in the importance of course sequencing among the ADs, the report concludes "the CCSS do not appear to figure prominently into states' current course sequencing discussions" (29). In their related report "Exploring the Use of Multiple Measures for Placement into College-Level Courses," released in 2014 and based on the a survey of ADs,

WestEd affirms research evidencing that standardized tests alone are not the best means for determining college admissions and placement (Bracco et. al). This is important given the research we previously detailed on the use of standardized tests for this purpose. The report discusses the range of measures in Core to College states that are being considered for college placement. Perhaps all we can take away from the WestEd studies of Core to College is that the effectiveness of Common Core State Standards in creating greater alignment and collaboration among K–12 and higher education is quite mixed. The mixed results of the Core to College initiative make it difficult to determine ongoing effects of this type of work. The Core to College initiative formally ended in 2014, although some states are certainly continuing this work and it will be important to see if it will lead to lasting and impactful K–12 and college collaborations. While we might be optimistic about the rich opportunities K–12 and college collaborations can yield, given how these efforts are being funded and how often they are used to establish ever greater systems of accountability and control over our K–12 classrooms, we must be cautious and critical optimists as we move forward.

All of this raises questions about who is driving U.S. higher education these days. Of course, higher education in the United States has always been shaped by multiple competing forces. For example, beginning in 1938 with Earnest Hollis' book *Philanthropy Foundations and Higher Education*, many researchers have documented the influence that private foundations have had on reforming higher education. In a study published in 2011 by Cassie Hall— using a review of academic literature, an analysis of public discourse from a wide variety of media, ten years of secondary data on philanthropic giving to higher education, and interviews with five senior-level professionals—Hall shows that there has been a fundamental shift in the relationship between foundations, higher education, and the control of public policy. Historically, foundations shaped higher education primarily through direct incentives to institutions with a focus on capital construction, academic research or programmatic efforts (Hall 16). But as Hall demonstrates in her analysis of the changing relationship between foundations and higher education, "recent foundation behavior suggests that a new approach to higher education philanthropy has emerged over the past decade, one that emphasizes broad-scale reform initiatives and systemic change through focused, hands-on public policy work" (2). This new approach to foundation work is being referred to as "advocacy philanthropy." Hall argues that foundations' "overt focus on public policy advocacy within specific state and local contexts will have a significant impact on higher education in the United States" (50).

As a conclusion to her study, Hall discusses the possible benefits, concerns, and emerging outcomes of this shift. Potential benefits of advocacy philanthropy include the attention foundations are drawing to important problems; creating a sense of urgency in the search for solutions; the effectiveness of grantmaking in bringing key actors together; and the ability of foundations to scale up reforms to achieve substantive change (96–100). Among the concerns are foundations' lack of external accountability and their concentration of power away from practice; the potential of their large-scale prescriptive grants to stifle innovation; and the extensive, perhaps excessive, influence gained by foundations through such advocacy (96–100). Emerging outcomes also raise issues to consider, such as diminishing funds available for field-initiated academic research, a shift from local focus to a national one that could affect changes to higher education power structures, and the lessening of trust in higher education institutions (83–92). Hall concludes, "the Bill and Melinda Gates Foundation and the Lumina Foundation for Education have taken up a set of methods—strategic grantmaking, public policy advocacy, the funding of intermediaries, and collaboration with government—that illustrate their direct and unapologetic desire to influence policy and practice in numerous higher education arenas" (109).

One of the areas in which Hall's concerns are most apparent is in how the Bill and Melinda Gates Foundation is funding the CCSS—our nation's first set of national standards marking perhaps one of the biggest public policy shifts in education to date. The analysis by Hall evidences that "college ready funding has been the largest funding priority for the Gates Foundation" (14). And when we refer to funding we are not talking about just the research, design, and implementation of the Standards, but also how they are funding support networks. For example, providing financial support to sites of the National Writing Project that agree to teach teachers how to meet CCSS, partnering with other foundations to support the Core to College initiative, founding the Collaborative for Student Success with other foundations whose sole purpose is to market the CCSS, and, more recently, funding Higher Ed for Higher Standards—a project of the Collaborative for Student Success designed to show that the CCSS are backed by our higher education leaders.

Understanding the role of accountability is crucial to the cautious and critically optimistic stance we take toward the CCSS and Core to College. Recognizing the competing forces at play, we see opportunity in the fact that for the first time, national standards have been established that attempt to put writing (and reading) on equal footing with science and math. We position ourselves as critical optimists because we believe the CCSS, while flawed, have value. Further, we hope that initiatives such as Core to College will lead to greater collaboration between high school and college faculty. However, as our historical sketch exhibits, at no other time have so many competing interests exerted such powerful and far-reaching force on U.S. classrooms in the name of accountability. And, our continued over-reliance on standardized testing is not only alarming, but also not producing the intended effects. As we chart a path forward, out next step must surely be to create opportunities to firmly establish student and teacher agency in the research, practice, and assessment of writing so that we can acknowledge the changes that need to be made to education without succumbing to the siren's call of crisis.

NOTES

1. As evidence of this increase we can look to the Collegiate Learning Assessment (CLA), which has grown the number of participating higher education institutions to 700 from its inception in 2002. Further, CAE (Council for Aid to Education), the organization that administers the CLA, is working with those developing Common Core State Standards Assessments to ensure alignment between their standardized tests and those used at the college level such as the CLA (Council for Aid to Education).

2. Throughout this book we focus on PARCC, but there is another consortium that has also developed CCSS aligned standardized tests—The Smarter Balanced Assessment Consortium. Because we don't intend this book to focus primarily on an analysis of these consortia, we chose to focus on PARCC as just one example of the current state of standardized testing in relationship to high school and college curricula both because it is the more controversial of the two consortia and because we both happen to live in PARCC member states.

3. Many historians agree that the first standardized tests to include writing were administered in China as early as 1115 A.D. These were known as "Imperial Examinations" and covered the Six Arts: music, math, writing, knowledge of the rituals of public and private life, archery, and horsemanship (Ward 44). The Imperial Examination was essentially a civil service exam that was open to nearly all males "and became the most important avenue to position, power, and prestige in China" (Hanson, 186).

4. For more on the role of the National Defense of Education Act on the shape of rhetoric and composition as a field, see Margaret Strain's "In Defense of a Nation: The National Defense Education Act, Project English, and the Origins of Empirical Research in Composition."

5. For more information, see http://www.learningoutcomesassessment.org/AboutUs.html.

6. For more information, see http://digitalcommons.unl.edu/peerreviewteaching/.

7. For a fuller discussion of the CCSS, see http://www.corestandards.org/about-the-standards.

CHAPTER 2

WRITING IN HIGH SCHOOL, WRITING IN COLLEGE

As detailed in the previous chapter, we find it interesting that measuring literacy growth remains such a conundrum for the United States. It has proven elusive enough that yearly tests of writing were not required under NCLB, long-term trends from NAEP show few significant gains, and the SAT plans to drop its required essay test. This has created significant openings for private testing companies and well-endowed private foundations to exert significant control over our public school system. If we look beyond the results of standardized tests, we see that this has also motivated significant research and evidence-based recommendations. Despite the sometimes contradictory and puzzling results, we find the turn toward this type of research both reaffirming and, at times, a cause for further alarm. Our goal in this chapter is to identify some of the most promising and problematic trends that persist across studies in order to better articulate what we know about literacy practices in high schools and colleges. Such articulations can be vitally important checks on an overreliance on standardized tests as we work to improve our ability to provide greater access to literacy across a variety of contexts.

While this overview is not exhaustive, it is representative and highlights emerging trends in large-scale writing research primarily over the past decade. In addition to discussing the research of others, we will also present the results of our own Conference on College Composition and Communication (CCCC) funded research, bringing the results of these major projects into conversation with one another as we set our sights on the future.

WRITING IN HIGH SCHOOL, WRITING IN COLLEGE

The research we have been conducting is supported by a grant from the CCCC, which describes the project's purpose as the creation of "an empirically-based description of student writing in high school and college settings." Our research is different from other similar studies in that we are gathering both direct and indirect evidence of how high school and college students and faculty experience writing instruction across the curriculum. Using a variety of measures, we strive to describe writing based on the experiences of both students and teachers by gathering evidence from a sample of schools and colleges that represent a diverse spectrum of educational institutions in the United States. To this end, our research includes three high schools and seven colleges/universities: one suburban public high school in a relatively affluent neighborhood (27 percent free/reduced lunch and 7 percent drop-out rate), one urban high school in a relatively poor neighborhood (63 percent free/reduced lunch and 26 percent drop-out rate), and one private, all-girls Catholic high school (free/reduced lunch and drop-out rate not tracked), as well as two community colleges, two four-year public institutions, one four-year private institution, one public master's-granting institution, and one doctorate-granting flagship institution.

We began with a survey of both faculty and students from across the curriculum (see Appendix A). The survey items were rooted in evidence-based best practices in writing instruction across the curriculum and reviewed by the CCCC's executive committee as part of their Research Initiative grant program. Doing survey research was the best option available for gathering information from a large number of participants across a broad spectrum of educational institutions in diverse geographical locations. Conducting survey research also allowed us to compare responses to the same questions across faculty and students from different types of institutions, as well as between faculty and students at the same and different institutions. Survey questions were designed to measure both the practice of writing by students and the teaching of writing practices by faculty. The questions were also designed to elicit multiple aspects of student and faculty perceptions about writing in college. Survey participants included 544 faculty and 1,412 students. The majors/departments of faculty and students ranged from industrial technology and religious studies to business and psychology. We then asked for volunteers among the survey participants to continue with us by completing an additional questionnaire and submitting a portfolio of all writing assigned or completed during the course of the semester. Twenty-one faculty and fourteen students from various institutions and departments participated in this phase. The response to this part of our research was not as high as we had hoped, and we plan to expand this phase in order to gather more direct evidence. In short, however, our research selects for a diversity of institutions, collects both direct and indirect evidence, includes an in-depth survey instrument, and compares answers to the same questions from both students and teachers in high school and college. Initial results from our research both confirm and complicate the findings of other large-scale projects.

CONSORTIUM FOR THE STUDY OF WRITING IN COLLEGE

One of the most important developments in large-scale writing research for our field is the recent partnership between the Council of Writing Program Administrators and the National Survey of Student Engagement (NSSE). Since 2000, NSSE has been offered as an alternative to popular rankings of colleges (e.g., the annual *U.S. News and World Report* college rankings). The primary goal of NSSE is to help faculty and students improve the undergraduate experience. As described on NSSE's homepage: "Survey items on The National Survey of Student Engagement represent empirically confirmed 'good practices' in undergraduate education. That is, they reflect behaviors by students and institutions that are associated with desired outcomes of college." Institutions that elect to participate in NSSE can use this survey of best practices to measure their own practices against similar institutions, as well as benchmarks established by NSSE. In 2007, the National Survey of Student Engagement and the Council of Writing Program Administrators entered into a formal collaboration. The most recent published results of that collaboration, which includes the twenty-seven questions on writing they developed, give us new cause to argue for the value of what faculty and students are doing in our writing classrooms. These questions were given to 23,000 students across the country and are rooted in research on best practices in writing instruction.[1]

NATIONAL COMMISSION ON WRITING

One of the most widely circulated research efforts comes from the National Commission on Writing (NCW), which was created by the College Board in 2002. As the College Board explains on the NCW website, while the commission was created in part because of College Board's plans to offer a writing assessment as part of the new SAT in 2005, "the larger motivation lay in the growing concern within the education, business, and policy-making communities that the level of writing instruction in the United States is not what it should be. Although there is much good work taking place in our classrooms, the quality of writing must be improved if students are to succeed in college and in life" (*The Neglected 'R'* 7). Among the many reports issued by the National Commission on Writing, we are primarily concerned with the results published in *Writing: A Ticket to Work . . . or a Ticket Out* and *Writing, Technology and Teens* (Lenhart, Arafeh, Smith, and Macgill). For the former report, the NCW sent a survey to the human resource directors of 120 major U.S. corporations affiliated with Business Roundtable. Combined, these corporations employ nearly eight million people. Survey results revealed that two-thirds of salaried employees in large U.S. companies have some writing responsibility, inadequate writing skills are a barrier to promotion, certain types of writing are commonly required, and an estimated $3 billion is spent each year training employees to write. The report *Writing, Technology and Teens* is a joint venture between the commission and the Pew Internet and American Life Project. Through telephone interviews and focus groups, this research seeks to understand the role writing plays in the lives of U.S. teens, and gathers their input on ways to improve school-based writing instruction.

NATIONAL CURRICULUM SURVEY

An organization similar to the College Board, ACT, Inc., administers the National Curriculum Survey every three to five years. This survey is far narrower in scope than those conducted by College Board. The National Curriculum Survey is sent to middle and high school teachers as well as college instructors who primarily teach introductory college-level courses. The goal of the survey is to collect information on what writing, reading, science, and math skills are expected of entering college students. Importantly, this research is also used to update common academic standards as well as ACT assessments, such as PLAN for tenth graders and the ACT for eleventh and twelfth graders.

INSTITUTIONALLY BASED RESEARCH

Although institutionally bound and currently limited to a very small range of institutions, longitudinal research on how students develop as writers at a single institution still has much to teach us. In particular we are referring to the Harvard Study of Writing (begun in 1997), the Stanford Study of Writing (begun in 2001), and the Longitudinal Study of Writing at the University of Denver (begun 2007). These studies trace large numbers of students over their academic careers, and sometimes beyond, providing very valuable local knowledge while also expanding knowledge in our discipline. For example, the Stanford Study of Writing "is a five-year longitudinal study investigating the writing practices and development of Stanford students during their undergraduate years and their first year beyond college in professional environments or graduate programs" ("About the Study"). Using a series of questionnaires over this five-year period, as well as interviews with a subgroup of students, researchers at Stanford hope not only to improve writing instruction at their local site, but also to make important contributions to longitudinal studies of writing development and writing across the curriculum.

The widely varying parameters of each of these studies and lack of access to raw data make it difficult to assert strong conclusions across all studies except in a few cases. Nonetheless, placing these studies in conversation with one another does allow us to draw valid inferences upon which to base ongoing research and plans for the future. In the following section we compare research results across the large-scale studies outlined above as we move toward articulating the trends, promises, and puzzles found not only in the results but in the research itself.

DEEP LEARNING AND WRITING INSTRUCTION

At its core, the National Survey of Student Engagement measures the extent to which institutions engage in practices that lead to high levels of student engagement. The results produced by NSSE have been used to establish a set of benchmarks for good educational practice at the college level. When the Council of Writing Program administrators joined forces with NSSE, they were seeking not only more information on writing instruction in the United States, but also an understanding of the extent to which engaging in certain types of writing instruction measures up to NSSE's benchmarks. Thus, the first set of responses to the writing-specific questions was used both to establish five scales that describe the quality of undergraduate writing and to establish that certain types of writing are "substantially related to NSSE's deep learning subscales,[2] especially higher-order thinking and integrative learning. . . . Taken together, these findings provide further support for the movement to infuse quality writing experiences throughout the curriculum" (22). The five scales are:

1. Pre-Writing Activities: How much feedback students received from faculty and others about their writing ideas and drafts.

2. Clear Expectations: How well instructors provided clear explanations of the goals and criteria of the writing assignments.

3. Higher-Order Writing: How often students wrote assignments involving summarization, analysis, and argument.

4. Good Instructor Practices: How much students collaborated with classmates, reviewed sample writing, and how often they were assigned practice writing tasks.

5. Integrated Media: How often students included numerical data, multimedia, and visual content in their writing. (22)

Table 2.1 displays how students responded to questions upon which the scales were built. It is no surprise to many that the five scales defined by NSSE are substantially related to their deep-learning subscales. What is important here is empirical confirmation by an independent organization of the value of much we already do.

Table 2.1 NSSE Results

From NSSE Table 9: Percent Responding "Some," "Most," or "All"
Assignments to Selected Writing Itemsₐ

	First-Year	Senior
For how many writing assignments have you:		
Talked with instructor to develop ideas before drafting	67%	67%
Received feedback from instructor about a draft	75%	63%
Received feedback from classmate, friend, or family about a draft	74%	64%
Visited campus-based writing center to et help	31%	19%
In how many writing assignments did you:		
Analyze or evaluate something you read, researched, or observed	91%	91%
Argue a position using evidence and reasoning	80%	73%
Explain in writing the meaning of numerical or statistical data	43%	50%
Create the project with multimedia web page, poster, etc.)	45%	68%
In how many writing assignments has your instructor:		
Explained in advance what he or she wanted you to learn	84%	82%
Explained in advance the grading criteria he or she would use	90%	91%
Asked you to do short pieces of writing that were not graded	54%	36%
Asked you to give feedback to a classmate about a draft	65%	38%

Response options included 1 = no assignments, 2 = few assignments, 3 = some assignments, 4 = most assignments, and 5 = all assignments. To view all 27 questions and their exact wording visit www.nsse.iub.edu/pdf/Writing_Questions_2008.pdf

As valuable as these insights are to writing studies in general, it is important to view these latest findings as one layer of data in relation to the many other studies that not only provide further support for these findings, but also expand upon and complicate them. For example, the 2002–2003 National Curriculum Survey administered by ACT, Inc., included responses from 1,099 college and 828 high school faculty in composition/language arts. Both high school faculty and college faculty ranked skills classified "writing as process" as more than moderately important, with the top three process or prewriting skills for both groups being "Selecting a Topic and Formulating a Thesis," "Editing and Proofreading," and "Revising Focusing on Content" rather than mechanics (9). Similarly, when ranking the most important purposes of writing, high school and college teachers agreed on four of the top five purposes: "developing logical arguments and supporting them with valid evidence," "writing an argumentative or persuasive essay," "writing expository prose," and "analyzing an issue or problem" (9). Similarly, in ACT's 2012 National Curriculum Survey, both high school English Language Arts (ELA) teachers and college composition teachers rated persuasive and informative/ explanatory texts as well as logical arguments as more important overall than poetry, journal entries, and narratives although the high school ELA teachers place a higher relative importance on writing such as poetry and journals than the college instructors (7).

This ranking of skills and purposes by faculty is in line with NSSE's deep-learning subscale. But in the ACT writing surveys, much like the NAEP questionnaires, even though faculty highly rank process-oriented writing instruction, we can't know what this means if the survey instrument is not detailed enough. As Applebee and Langer note in their analysis of NAEP results: "what teachers mean by this [process-oriented instruction] and how it is implemented in their classrooms remains unclear. The consistent emphasis that emerges in teachers' reports may mask considerable variation in actual patterns of instruction" ("The State of Writing Instruction" 26). This, of course, suggests a need for more in-depth studies that can unmask potential variations, such as the collaboration between the Center on English Learning and Achievement and the National Writing Project. But it also calls upon researchers to analyze raw data above and beyond that presented in final reports. For example, in taking a closer look at the ACT data, Patterson and Duer found a significant difference in the types of writing skills reportedly taught in classes of students identified as primarily college bound versus those who are primarily non-college bound (84–85). While the sample used to draw this conclusion is admittedly small, it does warrant a closer look at whether the persistence of tracking is contributing to the degree to which the achievement gap between students of different socioeconomic and racial groups also persists as identified by the NAEP.

The writing activities reported in the Stanford Study of Writing also closely reflect the kinds of activities associated with deep learning: "During their first year, students reported being assigned to do eighteen different kinds of writing; this broad range of genre persisted through the four years, though the ratio differed from year to year" (par. 1). As Figure 2.1 indicates, the majority of the kinds of writing students listed are also examples of higher-order writing indicated by the the NSSE deep-learning subscale.

Many of the initial results of our own research in this area are largely in line with these other results. Because our study varies from the NSSE/WPA collab-

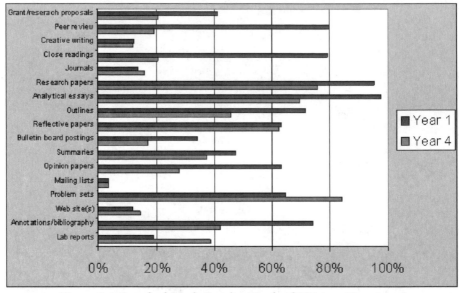

Figure 2.1 Stanford Study Results: Kinds of Writing–Year 1 to 4.

oration in terms of depth, we can offer results that extend, and sometimes challenge, these results as well as common current practices. Indeed, while at first glance the NSSE results and related research validates some of our work, a closer look complicates these findings in ways that call upon faculty and administrators to do more to promote deep learning using writing across the curriculum. For example, further investigation of the data shows that of the five scales developed by NSSE, there is significant adherence to, at best, only three (prewriting, clear expectations, and assigning higher-order writing) across the curriculum, and even these are subject to speculation.

In our own research, our goal has been to gather direct and indirect evidence of how both students and faculty experience writing instruction across the curriculum, beginning with a survey (see appendix) of both faculty and students. We did not have direct access to our survey respondents; all participating schools required that our survey be administered through the appropriate institutional research office. In some cases, the survey was distributed to all students and faculty on campus and in other cases to a representative sample of all students and faculty. Thus, determining an overall response rate is not possible and certainly a limitation. In our initial survey, 544 faculty and 1,412 students participated. Of the faculty, 22 percent were high school, 11 percent were community college, 19 percent were four-year public, 16 percent were four-year private, 8 percent were master's-granting public, and 24 percent were doctorate-granting public. Of the students, 13 percent were high school, 26 percent were community college, 6 percent were four-year public, 2 percent were four-year private, 8 percent were master's-granting public, and 47 percent were doctoral-granting public. Their majors/departments ranged from industrial technology and religious studies to business and psychology. The limitations our sample poses requires that our results be triangulated with the results of others as well as with a follow-up study of direct evidence.

Tables 2.2 and 2.3 focus on questions from our surveys related to prewriting, clear expectations, and good instructor practices (as defined by NSSE). It is interesting to note in these two tables the moments of convergence and divergence between high school and college faculty as well as faculty and students.

College and high school faculty across the curriculum are generally aligned with one another when it comes to prewriting, clear expectations, and good instructor practices. Most differences are relatively easy to explain. For example, while 58 percent of college faculty report sending students to institutional support services for writing, only 18 percent of high school faculty report doing so. This result may reflect that most U.S. high schools do not operate writing centers, instead relying on classroom teachers or paraprofessionals to do the work except in clearly defined circumstances (e.g., special education). We see two significant differences between college and high school faculty, however, that may merit further consideration: college faculty are far less likely than high school faculty to (1) provide opportunities for informal, exploratory writing or (2) have students read/respond to other students' work. Both of these components of literacy instruction are held in high esteem among writing specialists and reaffirmed by NSSE as activities that contribute to deep learning. Thus, while NSSE has identified common writing instruction practices related to deep learning, our results suggest that in at least these two areas of writing—exploratory writing and peer review—high school faculty may engage in a greater variety of writing activities that promote deep learning than college faculty. Of course, additional data is needed to more fully substantiate this claim.

The degree of alignment between high school and college faculty, or the fact that more high school faculty in our sample reported engagement in deep-learning activities than college faculty, may be surprising. What may be more (or less) surprising is the degree of similarity and difference between student and faculty responses at both levels. For example, while 30 percent of high school faculty report "always" requiring multiple drafts, only 16 percent

Table 2.2 College and High School Faculty Teaching Practices

Faculty Teaching Practice	Always	Some	Never
Require Multiple Drafts on Writing Assignments			
College Faculty	30	51	17
High School Faculty	30	50	16
Provide Written Feedback on Early Drafts		3	
College Faculty	47	38	12
High School Faculty	39	41	14
Conference with Students on Papers in Progress			
College Faculty	17	46	32
High School Faculty	31	40	23
Have Students Read/Respond to Other Students' Work			
College Faculty	19	36	41
High School Faculty	26	55	14
Provide Written Descriptions for Writing Assignments			
College Faculty	78	15	3
High School Faculty	67	25	5
Provide Grading Criteria Early in the Writing Process			
College Faculty	67	23	6
High School Faculty	63	28	7
Provide Opportunities for Informal, Exploratory Writing			
College Faculty	27	32	35
High School Faculty	40	39	12
Discuss Examples of Good Writing in Class			
College Faculty	44	41	13
High School Faculty	45	46	4
Discuss Writing with Your Class			
College Faculty	56	34	7
High School Faculty	60	39	4
Provide Handouts/Checklists/Examples			
College Faculty	54	34	9
High School Faculty	58	33	5
Provide References/Handbooks/Websites			
College Faculty	52	33	11
High School Faculty	36	42	17
Have Students Reflect on and Evaluate Own Writing			
College Faculty	223	339	33
High School Faculty	34	47	14

continued on next page

Table 2.2—*continued*

Faculty Teaching Practice	Always	Some	Never
Direct Students to Institutional Support Services for Writing (e.g., Writing Center)			
College Faculty	58	31	7
High School Faculty	18	29	47

Where the total percentage does not equal 100 participants, they either didn't respond or didn't know if they engaged in this particular activity as described in our survey.

Table 2.3 Teaching Practices and Corresponding Student Writing Activities

Teaching Practice | Student Writing Activity	Always	Some	Never
Require Multiple Drafts on Writing Assignments			
College Faculty	30	51	17
High School Faculty	30	50	16
Write Multiple Drafts			
College Students	28	48	16
High School Students	16	61	11
Conference with Students on Papers in Progress			
College Faculty	17	46	32
High School Faculty	31	40	23
Discuss Writing with My Teacher			
College Students	13	56	22
High School Students	12	58	15
Have Students Read/Respond to Other Students' Work			
College Faculty	19	36	41
High School Faculty	26	55	14
Discuss My Writing With Other Students			
College Students	12	53	26
High School Students	23	48	16
Direct Students to Institutional Support Services for Writing (e.g., Writing Center)			
College Faculty	58	31	7
High School Faculty	18	29	47

continued on next page

Table 2.3—*continued*

Teaching Practice | Student Writing Activity	Always	Some	Never
Discuss My Writing with the Writing Center or a Tutor			
College Students	3	22	65
High School Students	2	23	56
Provide References/Handbooks/Websites			
College Faculty	52	33	11
High School Faculty	36	42	17
Consult Reference Books, Handouts, Websites			
College Students	37	47	7
High School Students	24	46	13

of high school students report "always" writing multiple drafts. And while 31 percent of high school faculty report "always" conferencing with students on papers in progress, only 12 percent of high school students report "always" discussing their writing with their teacher. At the college level, while 58 percent of the faculty "always" direct students to institutional support services for writing, and 31 percent do so "sometimes," only 3 percent of students report "always" going to a writing center, and a small 22 percent "sometimes" seek institutional support services. These results and others suggest that even when faculty do engage in best practices for teaching writing, many students do not engage in best practices for learning how to write, calling attention to the need to find ways to encourage greater engagement among students for best practices in learning how to write.

One of the measures of the NSSE/WPA research that led to deep learning was clear expectations. We find this focus interesting given the wide variation in faculty and student rankings of writing abilities. If there is a high degree of clear expectations at play, should we not then expect student and faculty ranking of their writing abilities to be closely aligned? In our survey, faculty were asked to rank their students' writing abilities on a number of measures using a scale of 1–5 (1=very dissatisfied, 5=very satisfied). Students were asked to rank their own writing abilities using the same scale. Results are shown in Tables 2.4 and 2.5.

We asked faculty to rate how satisfied they are with students' ability on various markers of writing. For example, we asked them to rate how satisfied they are with students' ability to employ correct grammar and mechanics. The most highly satisfied faculty are those at the private high school, and the least satisfied are those at the urban high school. Also in the least-satisfied category are the

Table 2.4: Students' Writing Abilities as Ranked by Faculty

	Mean College Faculty Rating		Mean College Student Rating	
	Freshman/ Sophomore	Junior/ Senior	Freshman/ Sophomore	Junior/ Senior
Write appropriately for different audiences	2.66	2.97	3.66	4.03
Write appropriately for different purposes	2.52	2.93	3.83	4.18
Organize a paper	2.49	2.91	3.87	4.15
Develop a main idea	2.57	2.90	3.91	4.21
Use paragraphs appropriately	2.71	2.97	4.0	4.28
Use supporting evidence appropriately	2.43	2.77	3.87	4.29
Analyze data/ideas/arguments	2.20	2.73	3.81	4.19
Synthesize information from multiple sources	2.28	2.70	3.70	4.11
Appropriately use, cite and document sources	2.03	2.63	3.61	4.00
Quote and paraphrase appropriately	2.13	2.63	3.70	4.10
Record data and/or use detail	2.37	2.87	3.65	4.01
Use correct grammar and syntax	2.42	2.71	3.86	4.15
Employ correct mechanics (e.g., spelling)	2.39	2.85	3.96	4.19

Table 2.5: Students' Writing Abilities as Ranked by Themselves

	Mean High School Faculty Rating		Mean High School Student Rating	
	Freshman/ Sophomore	Junior/ Senior	Freshman/ Sophomore	Junior/ Senior
Write appropriately for different audiences	2.43	3.24	3.55	3.65
Write appropriately for different purposes	2.57	3.34	3.62	3.82
Organize a paper	2.69	3.25	3.73	3.81
Develop a main idea	2.83	3.36	3.67	3.84
Use paragraphs appropriately	2.75	3.36	3.71	4.10
Use supporting evidence appropriately	2.55	3.22	3.69	3.95
Analyze data/ideas/arguments	2.39	3.03	3.52	3.72
Synthesize information from multiple sources	2.20	2.78	3.38	3.64
Appropriately use, cite and document sources	2.18	2.92	3.56	3.71
Quote and paraphrase appropriately	2.14	2.97	3.51	3.85
Record data and/or use detail	2.41	3.04	3.56	3.70
Use correct grammar and syntax	2.52	3.11	3.60	3.80
Employ correct mechanics (e.g., spelling)	2.48	3.07	3.75	3.90

faculty at the community colleges and, perhaps surprisingly, the faculty at the doctorate-granting flagship university. Lumped in the middle are the four-year schools, the master's-granting university, and suburban public high school. It should be noted that on a scale of 1–5, with 1 being very dissatisfied and 5 being very satisfied, not a single faculty rated their students overall a 4 or 5—the highest average score was a 3.48 and the lowest a 1.92.

Students, however, think much more highly of their abilities than their teachers. Student overall ratings ranged from a low of 3.19 to a high of 4.3. Interestingly, student ratings of themselves at the private high school were most closely aligned with those of their teachers. Student ratings of themselves at the doctoral flagship university were least aligned with that of their teachers, followed closely by those at the urban high school. At the doctorate-granting institution, for example, faculty gave an overall score of 2.74 for student mastery of grammar, whereas the students gave themselves a 4.10. Several possible explanations could elucidate this disparity. One is that at this institution the highest percentage of students felt that their writing was equal to or better than that of their peers, thus indicating a generally higher self-perception of themselves as writers than students at other institutions or than their teachers feel is warranted. Of course, we might also want to consider class size (the smaller the class, the more direct communication between faculty and students, perhaps explaining why students at the private high school are most in line with their teachers). Further, it is possible that faculty have unrealistically high expectations for student writing. But in the end, we ask whether such great disparities in the rankings between faculty and students can exist if clear expectations for writing are set. Perhaps the self-reporting aspect of NSSE is suspect here, with the faculty choosing to respond to the questions on writing inflating the degree to which clear expectations are set. We hypothesize that the setting of clear expectations specifically for writing does not occur that often across the curriculum, thus leading to the disparity between faculty and student rankings. A study of direct evidence (e.g., actual faculty assignment sheets, peer review directions, etc.) is needed in order to begin to answer this question with any degree of validity.

BEYOND PREWRITING AND CLEAR EXPECTATIONS

NSSE's third scale is the degree to which faculty assign and students engage in higher-order writing. According to NSSE, the types of writing assignments that promote "deep learning" across the curriculum include those that focus on analysis, synthesis, and integration of ideas from various sources in ways that lead to engagement with course ideas both inside and outside of the classroom (22). But how much of the actual writing across the curriculum falls into this category?

Further, how does the writing assigned prepare students for writing beyond the academy? In large-scale studies, institutional studies, and our own research, it seems that much of the writing assigned to students across the curriculum does intend to promote deep learning, although very little prepares students for writing beyond the academy. For example, in 2003, Dan Melzer conducted textual analysis on 787 undergraduate writing assignments from forty-eight diverse academic institutions that were gathered via course websites. Melzer found, much like Britton in 1975 and Applebee in 1985, that the majority of the writing was transactional (84 percent), with almost half of the writing consisting of traditional essay exams, research papers, and journals.[3] In George Mason University's Faculty Survey of Student Writing, the three most important writing tasks included research paper (57 percent), critique or review (39 percent), and journal or other reflection paper (34 percent). Melzer's research confirms our own results that college faculty provide little opportunity for exploratory writing or workplace-based genres. As we reflect on the types of writing being assigned, we need to consider not only whether they promote deep learning, but also whether the writing submitted by students evidences the deep learning intended as well as ways in which we may or may not be preparing students for life beyond the academy.[4]

While our work here focuses on high school and college writing, we should still be very aware of the concerns raised by Applebee and Langer in their analysis of the most recent set of NAEP data in relation to K–8 writing instruction. Most notably, Applebee and Langer conclude that students are simply not writing enough to prepare them for the demands of postsecondary education. They highlight the fact that "some 40% of twelfth-grade students . . . report never or hardly ever being asked to write a paper of three pages or more" ("The State of Writing Instruction" 26). Not coincidentally, their analysis comes at the same time that influential educators and policymakers such as Dr. Diane Ravitch, former assistant secretary of education, professor at New York University and senior fellow at the Brookings Institution, and Chester E. Finn, former professor at Vanderbilt University and former assistant secretary of education, have begun to reverse course on the value of the No Child Left Behind Act, charter schools, and other similar efforts. As quoted in a *New York Times* article, Finn states: "Standards in many places have proven nebulous and low, . . . 'Accountability' has turned to test-cramming and bean-counting, often limited to basic reading and math skills" (Dillon). And, in our mind, too often ignoring the hard work of writing.

GENRES BEYOND THE UNIVERSITY

In *Writing: A Ticket to Work . . . or a Ticket Out,* the National Commission on Writing surveyed the Business Roundtable, an association of CEOs of many

63

leading U.S. corporations. Among the findings is that, "Writing is almost a universal professional skill required in service industries as well as finance, insurance, and real estate" (7). Upward of 70 percent of salaried employees have writing responsibilities. Indeed, 96–100 percent of the students and faculty at each school in our survey think writing will be somewhat important or very important to their future success, and 93–100 percent believe they will write often or very often after graduation. Here, it seems that our research agrees with the National Commission's. In our research, there is also significant consistency among students and faculty from all types of institutions about the role of writing in the workplace.

At this point we can share some useful information about the types of writing required in the workplace, college, and high school. In *Writing: A Ticket to Work . . . or a Ticket Out*, email and oral presentations with visuals aids such as PowerPoint are "frequently" or "almost always" required 80–98 percent of the time, followed by memos and official correspondence (70 percent), formal reports (62 percent), and technical reports (59 percent) (11). Similarly, in *Writing: A Powerful Message from State Government*, the National Commission on Writing's study of state government employees, email and memos/official correspondence are "frequently" or "almost always" required, followed by formal reports (71 percent), oral presentations (67 percent), technical reports (65 percent), legislative analysis (59 percent), and policy alerts (51 percent) (17).

But what do faculty view as the most important writing tasks? In our survey, high school faculty ranked the most important writing tasks assigned to freshman and sophomores as in-class writing, journal/reflective writing, and summary/abstract. At the junior/senior-level, high school faculty chose research paper, critique, position paper, and analysis paper. The data seem to suggest that high school faculty are following the lead of college faculty and working to prepare students for the types of writing they will encounter in college. But it may be that college faculty are not adequately preparing students for required writing tasks in the private or government sector. We doubt this is a matter of willful neglect on the part of faculty. After all, it would be as easy to assign memos as research papers.

Many faculty resist workplace genres on philosophical grounds, often arguing that their role is to help prepare citizens of the world, not train workers. While a student may never need to write an academic research paper in the workplace, many faculty believe the experience of doing so benefits students immensely when it allows for the opportunity to entertain an idea, follow its intellectual trajectory, and engage in its debate. Some research suggests that such noble goals, even if desirable, often are not met within the context of most

Table 2.6 Writing Tasks Assigned: College Faculty

Freshman/Sophomore		Junior/Senior	
Research Paper	34%	Research Paper	47%
Critique/Review Paper	27%	Analysis Paper	30%
Analysis Paper	27%	Critique/Review Paper	23%
Journal/Reflection Paper	24%	Reaction Paper	18%
Reaction Paper	21%	Position/Issue Paper	18%

writing assignments. Although we do not find the cultivating of critical citizens and productive workers to be mutually exclusive endeavors, we will sidestep this particular issue for now and focus on an emerging line of research that may help us better understand what is at stake. It has been posited by some that the abilities to analyze, synthesize, and integrate knowledge transfer across genres, thus making it less important to teach the genres of the workplace in the academy. Recent work by Elizabeth Wardle, David Smit, Anne Beaufort, Linda Bergman and Janet Zepernick, and others seeks to strongly draw our attention to the issue of transfer. In particular, they seek to understand whether the work students do in first-year composition courses transfers to other contexts, especially within the academy. Their attention to transfer comes on the heels of many studies strongly suggesting writing instruction is not preparing students for the literacy demands placed on them outside of school (Anson and Forsberg; Odell and Goswami; Spilka).

But given the research by members of our own field as well as those outside our field who have reached the same conclusions, alongside the findings of the National Commission on Writing, we must ask whether studying current practices for evidence of transfer is worthwhile. For example, it may be that issues of articulation and issues of transfer go hand-in-hand. In other words, growing evidence may suggest that what teachers and employers articulate as best practices in writing vary across discipline and context. Further, even within the same discipline, teachers may not be doing enough to articulate best practices to their students or employing the required meta-language as defined by Janet Giltrow, thus contributing to the disconnect we see in this data between students and teachers. If there is a problem of articulation, then a valid study of transfer must also take into account matters of articulation. As a step in this direction, we suggest that rhetoric and composition as a field must establish a framework for the literacy demands in academia and beyond, to which the work completed in first-year writing courses must aspire, all the while being grounded in the rich rhetorical tradition that reaches back thousands of years.

WRITING ATTRIBUTES BEYOND THE UNIVERSITY

In addition to genre, we have evidence of the *value* that employers, faculty, and students place on certain aspects of writing. In the National Commission on Writing report, 96 percent of employers view *accuracy* as "extremely important" or "important," 97 percent view *clarity* as "extremely important" or "important," and 95 percent view *spelling, punctuation, and grammar* as "extremely important" or "important" ("Writing: A Ticket to Work" 28). In our survey, faculty were asked to identify the five most important characteristics of good writing in their field. Interestingly, as Figure 2.2 indicates, among college faculty, organization was chosen more often than any other characteristic (66 percent), followed closely by analysis data/ideas/arguments (59 percent), and uses supporting evidence appropriately (57 percent). Because organization is a major contributor to clarity, and both analysis and use of evidence constitute accuracy, these findings align with one another.

We are struck by the interesting lack of focus on audience and purpose by faculty in the disciplines—especially given the emphasis that rhetoric, composition, and our textbooks place on it. This result could be explained by faculty's lack of awareness of the role that audience and purpose play in helping a writer make sound rhetorical choices; thus, if a paper is well organized, it is "readable" by the audience and supports its purpose nearly invisibly. However, given the amount of transactional writing found by Melzer that, by definition, has audience as one of its primary foci, it could be that faculty across the curriculum do care quite a bit about audience, but have not articulated it in the ways we do in composition. This finding is worth further exploration.

We'd like to end our look at the survey results on a truly affective note. After all, if people just do not like to write, we have an entirely different battle to wage. In some ways, the results of the data are not surprising. As Table 2.7 indicates, nearly half of the high school students reported that they enjoyed writing for their own personal goals, but disliked assigned school writing. What is perhaps surprising is that 41 percent of college students reported that they enjoy writing and look forward to most writing tasks, whereas only 28 percent of high school students felt that way.

Numerous reasons could exist for this change over time. As students progress through college, they perhaps gain more confidence as writers (indeed 56 percent of college students felt that they write as well as or better than their peers), and a more confident writer is one who can approach a new writing task without apprehension. It may also be that college students have been writing more—since elementary school perhaps, or since high school certainly—and they have simply gained more experience with it. With more experience, they

Table 2.7 Students' Affective Response to Writing and Their Abilities

	College Students	High School Students
I enjoy writing and look forward to most writing tasks	41	28
I enjoy writing for personal goals but do not like school-related writing	36	48
I do not like to write	16	13
I think I write as well or better than most of my peers	56	30
I think I write about the same as my peers	25	39
I think most of my peers write better than I do	7	12
I think almost all of my peers write better than I do	1	1
I don't know how my writing compares to my peers		6

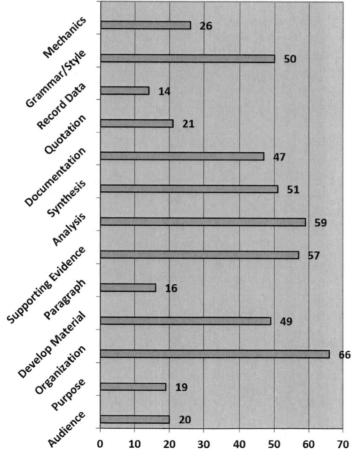

Figure 2.2: College Faculty Views of Good Writing in the Disciplines

have confidence that they can meet the goals of a new writing situation. Alternatively, as found in the Pew Internet and American Life/National Commission on Writing report, *Writing, Teens, and Technology,* part of the story is that what teenagers define as writing is not nearly as inclusive as what we might define as writing (Lenhart et al.). In other words, the teens in this survey did not consider what we in rhetoric and composition would call digital or multimodal writing (emails, blogging, texting, and the like) as writing. Thus, teenagers may actually be writing more than ever, but in a far greater variety of forms not normally recognized as part of the school or work experience. These results, which are worthy of further exploration but beyond the scope of this volume, do leave us with a positive note: for our students, writing is not necessarily the "dreaded" activity that many of us imagine.

NOTES

1. The WPA/NSSE collaboration is now known as the Consortium for the Study of Writing in College, and a list of the questions administered can be found at http://comppile.org/wpa+nsse/docs/27_Question_Supplement.pdf.

2. A significant body of scholarship has addressed the concepts of deep learning. According to Thomas Laird, Michael Schwarz, Rick Shoup, and George Kuh, "students who use deep approaches to learning tend to perform better as well as retain, integrate, and transfer information at higher rates than students using surface approaches to learning" (3). To measure deep learning, NSSE uses three subscales: higher-order learning, integrative learning, and reflective learning. NSSE acknowledges that the questions in each subscale are not "intended as a replacement for other, more in-depth measures of deep learning; it [the instrument] serves as a quick way to address this important concept in a survey that reaches a substantial number of college students every year" (Laird, Shoup, and Kuh).

3. Melzer categorized writing samples following the research of James Britton: "Britton divided writing into three different "functions," which correspond to different points on the rhetorical triangle of writer (the expressive function), text (the poetic function), and audience (the transactional function). Transactional assignments ask students to inform or persuade an audience; for example, a book review, annotated bibliography, or editorial. Expressive assignments are informal and exploratory, with minimal demands for structure and the self as audience. Freewrites and personal journals are typical expressive assignments. Poetic writing is imaginative, with the focus on the text itself as an art form. Poems, stories, and plays are common poetic assignments. Based on Timothy Crusius' (1989) critique of Britton's categories, which Crusius feels lack a place for informal writing for an audience beyond the self, I added one more category, "exploratory." Like expressive assignments, exploratory

assignments are informal and focus on exploring ideas, but the audience is public and the form is usually more structured than expressive assignments" (Melzer 88).

4. That college should be preparing students for their professional lives is certainly a debate that can be traced back at least to the Morrill Act about the value of higher education in general and a student's purpose in attending university. We do not dismiss the intrinsic value of education to broaden one's mind and engage deeply with new ideas. Nor do we think that the writing courses should be limited in scope to providing a service to the university and its students: gaining rhetorical awareness and sophistication promotes engaged citizenry and academic success. In today's economies of academia and the world, scholars and teachers cannot blindly ignore that students, parents, taxpayers, and legislators believe that a higher education in general is a way to a better life and job.

APPENDIX A: STUDENT SURVEY OF WRITING IN COLLEGE

1. Your gender:
- ☐ Female
- ☐ Male

2. How old are you? _____

3. Currently I am:
- ☐ A first or second-year college student
- ☐ A community college student for more than one year
- ☐ A junior or senior college student at a 4-year school

4. Which kind of high school did you attend?
- ☐ Public
- ☐ Private

5. How many years of English did you take in high school?
- ☐ 1
- ☐ 2
- ☐ 3
- ☐ 4

6. Have you taken other kinds of writing classes, such as journalism, creative writing, or any other kind of course in which a primary focus was writing?
- ☐ No
- ☐ Yes. Name of course(s):

7. Which of the following kinds of writing tasks do you recall doing during high school in any kind of class? (Some answers will overlap. Please check as many as apply.)

- ☐ Research paper
- ☐ Essay exam answers
- ☐ Personal narrative (a nonfiction piece about yourself)
- ☐ Essay
- ☐ An obituary
- ☐ A poem
- ☐ Analysis of a poem, story, or other reading
- ☐ Short story
- ☐ Newspaper article or letter to the editor
- ☐ Speech
- ☐ Argumentative paper
- ☐ Lab report
- ☐ Summary
- ☐ Evaluation
- ☐ Journal or other reflective writing
- ☐ Professional letter
- ☐ Issue paper
- ☐ Collaborative (or group) paper
- ☐ Other (please specify): _____

8. When you wrote papers in your English classes, did you get written feedback from your teacher about the quality of the paper?

- ☐ Yes
- ☐ No

9. Did you usually receive a grade for the paper?

- ☐ Yes
- ☐ No

10. In your best estimate, how often did you have writing tasks/assignments in classes other than English?

- ☐ Often
- ☐ Occasionally
- ☐ Rarely
- ☐ Never

11. If you wrote in other classes, what classes did you write in? (Check as many as apply.)

- ☐ History
- ☐ Science
- ☐ Math

- ☐ P.E.
- ☐ Civics
- ☐ Geography
- ☐ Health
- ☐ Foreign Language
- ☐ Other (please specify): _____

12. When you produced writing in other classes, did you get written feedback from your teacher about the quality of the paper?

- ☐ Yes
- ☐ No

13. Did you usually receive a grade for the writing?

- ☐ Yes
- ☐ No

The following questions will ask about your overall experiences and attitudes about writing.

14. How important do you think writing is to your future job or career?

- ☐ Very important
- ☐ Somewhat important
- ☐ Neither important nor unimportant
- ☐ Not very important
- ☐ Don't know

15. How often do you think you will have to write after you finish high school?

Very often   Often   Rarely   Never

16. How would you characterize your feelings about writing? (Choose the answer that is the closest match to your feelings.)

- ☐ I enjoy writing and look forward to most writing tasks.
- ☐ I enjoy writing for personal goals but do not like school-related writing.
- ☐ I do not like to write.

17. Which of these responses best matches your perception of your writing ability?

- ☐ I think I write as well or better than most of my peers.
- ☐ I think I write about the same as my peers.
- ☐ I think most of my peers write better than I do.
- ☐ I think almost all of my peers write better than I do.
- ☐ I don't know how my writing compares to my peers.

18. How much emphasis do you think your school places on writing?

- ☐ Too much
- ☐ Enough
- ☐ Not enough
- ☐ Don't know

19. How satisfied are you with your ability to:

	Very dissatisfied				Very satisfied
Write appropriately for different audiences	●	●	●	●	●
Organize a paper	●	●	●	●	●
Develop a main idea	●	●	●	●	●
Use paragraphs appropriately	●	●	●	●	●
Use supporting evidence	●	●	●	●	●
Analyze ideas/arguments/data	●	●	●	●	●
Synthesize information from multiple sources	●	●	●	●	●
Appropriately use, cite, and document sources	●	●	●	●	●
Quote and paraphrase appropriately	●	●	●	●	●
Record data and/or use appropriate level of detail	●	●	●	●	●
Use correct grammar and syntax	●	●	●	●	●
Employ correct mechanics (spelling and punctuation)	●	●	●	●	●

20. To what extent do you engage in the following strategies when writing?

	Always use	Some-times use	Never use	Don't know
Write multiple drafts	●	●	●	●
Discuss my writing with my teacher	●	●	●	●
Discuss my writing with the Writing Center or a tutor	●	●	●	●
Discuss my writing with other students (including peer review)	●	●	●	●
Discuss my writing with someone other than my teacher or tutor	●	●	●	●
Consult reference books or websites	●	●	●	●

The following questions will ask about your experiences writing in college.

21. Did you take a freshman composition course at this or another institution?
- ☐ Yes
- ☐ No

22. Have you taken any other kind of course that focuses on writing at this or another institution?
- ☐ No
- ☐ Yes. Type of course: _____

23. Have you taken other English classes?

☐   Yes

☐   No

24. As you reflect upon your college experience, how often did you have to write in courses outside of English?

☐   In most courses

☐   In some courses

☐   In a few courses

☐   Never

25. If you wrote in other classes, what classes did you write in? (Check as many as apply.)

☐   History

☐   Science

☐   Math

☐   Psychology

☐   Economics

☐   Education

☐   Business

☐   Engineering

☐   Geography

☐   Philosophy

☐   Anthropology

☐   Sociology

☐   Social Work

☐   Speech

☐   Health Sciences/Nursing

☐   Foreign Language

☐   Professional field/Other (please specify): _____

26. What kinds of writing did you have to produce? (Some answers will overlap. Please check as many as apply.)

☐   Summary and/or analysis

☐   Abstract or precis

☐   Research paper

☐   Lab report

☐   Personal opinion paper

☐   Annotated bibliography

☐   News stories and/or press releases

☐   Essay exam answers

☐   Case study and/or narratives

☐   Journals and/or other reflection papers

- ☐ Impromptu in-class writing
- ☐ Reaction paper
- ☐ Outline writing
- ☐ Critiques, evaluations, or reviews
- ☐ Professional letters and/or memos
- ☐ Literature review
- ☐ Collaborative (or group) project
- ☐ Analysis of a poem, story, or other reading
- ☐ Other (please specify): _____

27. Did your professors give you guidelines about how to write in various disciplines?
- ☐ Yes
- ☐ No

28. Other than English classes, did your professors devote class time to discussing the paper, giving advice about how to write it, or the like?
- ☐ In most courses
- ☐ In some courses
- ☐ In a few courses
- ☐ Never

29. When you produced writing in other classes, did you get written feedback from your teacher about the quality of the paper?
- ☐ Yes
- ☐ No

30. Did you receive a grade on the writing?
- ☐ Yes
- ☐ No

CHAPTER 3

WHAT'S AN ADMINISTRATOR OR TEACHER TO DO?

Repeatedly we have found that students, teachers, parents, and employers all view the ability to write well as a highly valuable skill. For example, Harvard's Professor of Education Richard J. Light, in his study *Making the Most of College*, found: "Of all skills students say they want to strengthen, writing is mentioned three times more than any other" (54). The alumni surveyed as part of Light's study also regard writing as extremely important, as more than 90 percent designated "need to write effectively" an ability "of great importance" in their jobs. And, *Writing: A Ticket to Work . . . or a Ticket Out"* the National Commission on Writing's report, sponsored by College Board, concluded:

> Writing appears to be a "marker" attribute of high-skill, high-wage, professional work. This is particularly true in sectors of the economy that are expanding, such as services, and the finance, insurance, and real estate sectors. Educational institutions interested in preparing students for rewarding and remunerative work should concentrate on developing graduates' writing skills. Colleges and university leaders, as well as school officials, should take that advice to heart. The strength of corporate complaints about the writing skills of college graduates was surprisingly powerful. (19)

Additionally, in a more recent survey conducted in 2011, researchers from Michigan State University in collaboration with the Association of Public Land Grant Universities and the University Industry Consortium identified the important soft skills needed as students transfer from college to employment in agriculture, natural resources, and related careers. The 8,000-plus students, faculty, alumni, and employers who participated in this survey ranked communication skills as the highest priority, with "effective written communication" and the ability to "communicate appropriately and professionally using social media" as among the highest of these skills (Crawford et al. 9).

And yet, as Laura Cutler and Steve Graham remind us when asking why writing has not received the same attention as reading or math:

> One thing is for certain: It is not because students are developing the writing skills they need to be successful. Take for instance the findings of the most recent National Assess-

ment of Educational Progress (NAEP) (Persky, Daane, and Jen, 2003). The writing of two-thirds or more of the students tested in Grades 4, 8, and 12 was below grade-level proficiency. . . . Just as importantly, many youngsters leave high school lacking the writing skills needed for success in college or the world of work. College instructors estimate that 50% of high school graduates are not prepared for college-level writing demands (Achieve, Inc., 2005), whereas businesses in the United States spend $3.1 billion annually for writing remediation (National Commission on Writing, 2004). (907)

Answers to the question of why writing has been largely absent from the school reform movement are varied and complicated. Perhaps most notable at this moment is the elusiveness of large-scale measures of writing achievement that can lead to a recursive process of improvement, and that the high-stakes tests used to determine curricula in school districts everywhere, with their focus primarily on math and reading, have resulted in driving writing out of the classroom (Applebee, "Great Writing"). However, the Common Core State Standards, with an emphasis on literacy across the curriculum, may provide us with an opportunity to dramatically alter the status of writing in U.S. classrooms.

Despite all of this, numerous studies conducted by a variety of stakeholders in different contexts reach surprisingly similar conclusions about the path forward, and in this chapter we lay the foundation for that path through a synthesis of the recommendations of these stakeholders. In short, results repeatedly show that our efforts should be focused on three related areas: writing across the curriculum, effective and responsive instruction, and professional development. Interwoven throughout discussions of these key areas is assessment. Because the most highly effective forms of assessment stand in a recursive relationship to writing across the curriculum, instruction, and professional development, we don't treat it as a separate area but rather one that must be interwoven within these three.

For example, returning to our touchstone year of 2006, the National Commission on Writing's report, *Writing and School Reform* combines the results of five hearings held at different locations throughout the United States (Office of the National Association of State Universities and Land-Grant Colleges, Haas Foundation, Alcorn State University, Annual Convention of the National Council of Teachers of English (NCTE), and the University of Texas). Attendees included teachers, principals, superintendents, state department of education officials, curriculum coordinators, two- and four-year college and university faculty, admissions directors, program heads and department chairs, deans, provosts and presidents, and officers and staff of national education associations. This diverse group reached far-ranging consensus on the path forward. As can be seen in Table 3.1, the points of consensus with a checkmark generally fall into one of the three areas we list above—writing across the curriculum, effective and responsive instruction, and professional development.

Table 3.1 Points of Consensus About Writing Needs. Source: National Commission on Writing, Writing and School Reform.

Recommendations: The Neglected "R"	Consensus Agreement During Hearings
A Writing Agenda that Includes:	
Comprehensive writing policy in state standards	✓
Doubling the amount of time spent writing	✓
Additional state and local financial support	✓
Writing in all subjects and all grade levels	✓
Required writing preservice for teaching license	✓
A white House Conference on Writing	
Improved writing instruction for undergraduates	✓
Time	
Double the amount of time students spend writing	✓
Double resources devoted to writing instruction	
Assign writing across the curriculum	✓
Encourage out-of-school writing	✓
Encourage Parents to review children's writing	
Teachers and Professional Development	
Requirement of writing across subjects and grades	✓
Developmentally appropriate writing for all students, from kindergarten through college	✓
Common expectations for writing across disciplines	
In-service workshops to help teachers understand writing and develop as writers	✓
Professional development for university faculty to improve student writing	
University-school partnerships to improve writing for English-language learners	✓

continued on next page

Table 3.1—*continued*

Recommendations: The Neglected "R"	Consensus Agreement During Hearings
Technology	
Create a National Educational Technology Trust to finance technology and training	
Employ technology to help improve writing	✓
Apply technology to the grading and assessment of writing	
Measuring Results	
Assessment of writing competence must be fair and authentic	✓
Standards, curriculum, and assessment must be aligned in reality as well as in rhetoric	
Assessments of student writing must go beyond multiple-choice, machine-scored items	✓
Assessment should provide students with adequate time to write	✓
Assessment should require students to actually create a piece of prose	
Best writing assessment should be more widely replicated	✓

That such a diverse group could reach this level of consensus in 2006 is an early sounding of the work to follow, reaching similar conclusions. Of note is that "Standards, curriculum, and assessment must be aligned in reality as well as rhetoric" was not a point of consensus during the hearings, and yet now it is exactly the focus of so much time, money, and debate as discussed in Chapters One and Two.

WRITING ACROSS THE CURRICULUM (WAC)

Literacy researchers have long argued that writing is not a single, generalizable skill that can be learned outside a social or disciplinary framework. While there seem to be some skills that we can teach students to transfer across contexts, each new context will present new challenges and ways of seeing and writing that can only be learned when immersed in that context. In short, the central argument for enhanced writing across the curriculum is that "for students to become successful, capable writers . . . requires a protracted period of time during which they encounter many opportunities to write and receive feedback in multiple contexts" (Johnson and Krase 32).

It is not surprising that the history of writing across the curriculum in America parallels that of the history of standardized writing tests. While many point to the late 1970s/early 1980s as the beginning of WAC as a subfield of composition studies, much like standardized writing tests, its roots go back to the beginning of the modern U.S. university. As previously discussed, early U.S. universities were populated by students who reliably absorbed social, political, and academic values and positions similar enough that their linguistic homogeneity meant there was no need to teach writing out of context. The huge increase, and relative diversity, of students who began to enter the university in the mid-1800s, as well as the new value placed on specialized knowledge and the separation of academic disciplines, changed all of this. In tracing the history of writing across the curriculum, David Russell explains, "almost from the beginning of the modern university, critics from many quarters attacked academic specialization and the relegation of responsibility for writing instruction to the English department" (56). Indeed, Russell points to the work of John Dewey, Fred N. Scott, James Fleming Hosic, Joseph Denney, and others in demonstrating very early efforts to "promote interdepartmental cooperation in teaching language" (60).

While current implementations of writing across the curriculum vary greatly, the central tenets are widely agreed upon:

- Instruction in writing should include the production of a wide array of texts.
- We cannot assume automatic transfer of general writing skills taught in freshman composition courses or the humanities in general.
- The ability to write in discipline-specific genres is central to gaining access to specialized discourse communities.
- Learning how to write in one's discipline shouldn't be a process of trial and error, but rather a structured, guided process that builds on transferable skills and knowledge as well as expands to include discipline-specific literacy skills.
- Writing can be used to promote learning.
- Writing can be used to assess learning.
- Writing can increase student engagement with course material.

For too long these tenets and calls for increased use of writing across the curriculum have required us to act on faith supported by little empirical evidence. For example, in the National Commission on Writing's reports *The Neglected R* and *Writing and School Reform*, the commission found broad support from parents, teachers, and administrators for writing across the curriculum:

> Too frequently, writing is seen as an academic skill that is the responsibility of English or language arts teachers. Insisting on the widespread use of writing across curriculum areas, includ-

ing mathematics and science, holds the promise of improving students' writing competence, deepening subject-matter
knowledge, and expanding the amount of time students
spend writing. (*The Neglected R* 25)

The "promise" of improving students' writing through writing across the
curriculum programs, even in this report, has not been strongly supported by
empirical evidence until very recently. Further, it is likely that this lack of evidence has contributed to the relatively slow growth of strong implementation of
writing across the curriculum at all levels and through our national, state, and
local assessments of academic achievement.

One important advance in this area is the collaboration between NSSE and
WPA. In 2009 the Consortium for the Study of Writing in College (a collaboration between the Writing Program Administrator's Council and the National
Survey of Student Engagement) released a report detailing the purpose and results of the WPA/NSSE survey:

At the inter-institutional and national levels, little data affirm
writing specialists' widespread belief that writing-to-learn
activities improve learning, engagement, and attainment.
Therefore, in 2008, we administered 27 supplemental NSSE
questions about writing practices to 23,000 students in 82
randomly selected four-year institutions, providing the broadest snapshot so far of undergraduate writing. . . . [In results
from across the curriculum] writing assignments encouraged
interactive writing activities (peer response, teacher response,
visits to a writing center, etc.), specified "meaning-constructing
writing" (synthesizing information, writing to a specific
audience), and included clear explanations of the instructor's
expectations. Controlling for student characteristics (gender, race, major, and others) and the amount students wrote,
results show that more work in these areas are associated with
more engagement in deep learning activities and greater self-
reported gains in practical competence, personal and social
development, and general education. (Anderson, et al. 1)

More recently, individual researchers have begun to publish compelling results on discrete aspects of writing across the curriculum that can help us build
more complex levels of evidence on the effectiveness of an approach so many call
for as one of the most promising ways to improve student writing. For example,
Christopher Wolfe identifies argument as one of the primary genres employed

across the curriculum. After examining 265 undergraduate writing assignments from seventy-one courses across the curriculum at his university, he found that 59 percent of the assignments required argumentation. However, it was very clear that the different academic contexts Wolfe analyzed required different forms of argumentation. Juxtaposing the work of Stephen Toulmin, Aaron A. Larson, and others with the actual assignments given to students, Wolfe identified the seven different kinds of arguments used in different academic situations:

- The explicitly thesis-driven assignment
- Text-centered arguments
- Mixed-genre argument
- Empirical arguments
- Decision-based arguments
- Proposals
- Compound arguments

This type of discrete research is an important step in the development of writing across the curriculum because, as Wolfe notes:

> Students are learning a great deal about how to write in their humanities courses, including argumentative writing—but relatively little about how to make empirical arguments, decision-based arguments, and some other kinds of arguments prized in different disciplines. Understanding both similarities and differences among disciplines is key to developing more effective programs in writing across the curriculum." (208)

This is an extension of ACT's finding in their 2012 report that "in their focus on literary content knowledge, high school literature and reading courses may not be well aligned with college expectations" in terms of the range of the actual types of writing required of students both in college-level writing courses and across the curriculum (9). Further, this points to an emerging area of research that may be key to the interdepartmental work of writing instruction, *transfer*, a topic we will explore more fully in Chapter Four.

Finally, while the participation of the Bill and Melinda Gates Foundation in these debates is relatively new, their broad coalitions, deep pockets, and support for the Common Core State Standards may have the largest effect on writing across the curriculum and a realignment of the reading/writing hierarchy we have ever seen. The foundation's 2010 report *Supporting Instruction: Investing in Teaching* makes their position clear:

Literacy improves as students read and write about a range of increasingly complex texts. Outside of English language arts (ELA), there are rarely classes in middle or high school that focus just on literacy. Indeed, the Common Core State Standards expect literacy instruction to be included in a number of subjects outside of ELA, including science and social studies/history. The standards focus especially on connecting reading and writing, emphasizing nonfiction reading as well as writing that offers a clear analysis based on evidence—the kind of literacy students need to succeed in college and the workplace.

While a majority of stakeholders are quite vocal about the need to strengthen writing across the curriculum if we are to meet the needs of twenty-first century learners, they are equally silent on how to pay for it. As Les Perelman explains in describing the long-standing and highly successful WAC program at MIT, "the program is valued across MIT because it is funded sufficiently to make a difference to faculty." To show us what this means, he reveals that MIT has thirty-six full and part-time lecturers, at an expense equivalent to the cost of nineteen assistant professors in the humanities, working with an undergraduate population of just over 4,000 students. In short, if the promise of writing across the curriculum is to be realized, it must not come in the form of add-on writing intensive credit hours or the assignment of underpaid and undertrained teaching assistants to courses in the disciplines. For a WAC program to be successful, someone must be willing to pay for it. As shown in previous chapters, the Bill and Melinda Gates Foundation is willing to pay for significant parts of such efforts if they are aligned with CCSS. And while we certainly support the emphasis on writing across the curriculum and the promise CCSS holds in this regard, we have significant concerns about the concentration of power, accountability, and control currently being exercised by advocacy philanthropists in regard to our public school system.

EFFECTIVE AND RESPONSIVE INSTRUCTION

The second of the three widely agreed upon keys to establishing an educational reform focus on writing is not only to call for effective and responsive instruction and assessment, but to begin establishing benchmarks and models for what this looks like. Of course, given the often dramatic diversity of learners we work with every day, it is impossible to declare any one single approach to writing instruction as *the* most effective way to teach writing. However, more and more research shows us that instructional practices, writing genres, and assessments "should be *holis-*

tic, authentic, and *varied"* (NCTE, *Writing Now*). While this advice has, for too long, appeared subjective and unproven, the last several years have witnessed an increase in research that shows us just what this means. For example, when the WPA partnered with NSSE in 2008 to form the Consortium for the Study of Writing, administering the supplemental questions on writing to 23,000 students in eighty-two randomly selected four-year institutions, they were able to identify five activities that highly correlated with NSSE's deep learning scales of higher order thinking, integrative learning, and reflective learning. The five activities include:

1. Pre-Writing Activities: How much feedback students received from faculty and others about their writing ideas and drafts.
2. Clear Expectations: How much instructors provided clear explanations of the goals and criteria of the writing assignments.
3. Higher-Order Writing: How frequently students wrote assignments involving summarization, analysis, and argument.
4. Good Instructor Practices: How much students collaborated with classmates, reviewed sample writing, and engaged in practice-writing tasks.
5. Integrated Media: How much students included numerical data, multimedia, and visual content in their writing. (NSSE)

In their 2009 presentation at the WPA conference, consortium members Paul Anderson, Chris Anson, Bob Gonyea, and Chuck Paine detailed the types of higher order writing activities that are aligned with deep learning across the curriculum:

> ANALYZING the basic elements of an idea, experience, or theory, such as examining a particular case or situation in depth and considering its components
>
> SYNTHESIZING and organizing ideas, information, or experiences into new, more complex interpretations and relationships
>
> MAKING JUDGMENTS about the value of information, arguments, or methods, such as examining how others gathered and interpreted data and assessing the soundness of their conclusions
>
> APPLYING theories or concepts to practical problems or in new situations

It was during this same time frame that the National Council of Teachers of English published *Writing Now*. After synthesizing the results of numerous research studies, NCTE offered the following benchmarks independently of the research conducted by the National Commission on Writing and the Consortium for the Study of Writing, again showing a high level of agreement among different stakeholders:

For Teachers:

- Require all students—especially the less experienced ones—to write extensively so that they can be comfortable writing extended prose in elementary school, and a minimum of five-page essays in high school and ten-page essays in college.
- Create writing assignments that ask students to interpret and analyze in a wide variety of genres.
- Employ functional grammar approaches to help students understand how language works in a variety of contexts.
- Foster collaborative writing processes.
- Make new-media writing part of students' regular composing.
- Use strategies of formative assessment to give students feedback on developing drafts.
- Employ multiple measures, including portfolios, to provide summative assessments of students' development as writers.

For Schools

- In hiring instructors, be sure that their professional education has included coursework in writing instruction.
- Develop authentic assessments of writing that bridge the gaps between school and workplace writing, and be sure to include multiple measures of writing proficiency, such as portfolios.
- Create curricula that foster writing in every subject at every grade level.
- Build a technological infrastructure to support new media writing.
- Invest in professional development for writing instructors.

For Policymakers

- Develop programs for professional development in writing instruction for teachers at all levels.
- Encourage and fund studies that bridge the gaps between qualitative and quantitative research on writing; between research in composition studies and in teacher education; between school and workplace writing; and among writers at varying developmental and skill levels.
- Provide funding for both technological and professional development support of new-media writing.

How	Writing is most effectively taught as a process of differentially employed strategies. Multiple points of feedback from teachers and peers both in class and outside of class is a crucial component of the formative assessment that can lead to success. Functional, not prescriptive, grammar, mechanics, and style should be practiced through proven techniques such as sentence combining. Multiple measures of formative and summative assessment should be used. Ample time should be spent reading and analyzing model writing from all disciplines.
What	Students must be given the time to write in the multiple genres they will encounter most frequently in college and in the workplace, with an emphasis on synthesis, analysis, and argument. ELA in high school and college should focus less on literary content knowledge and more on applying literary analytical techniques to a range of texts across disciplines and careers. In high school, students should be required to produce extended writing with a focus on depth. Opportunities to apply theories or strategies to practical problems should be made available. The gap between school, home, and workplace writing must be effectively bridged.
Where	Writing must not be seen as the sole province of literature teachers in English departments. Instead, English departments at all levels should embrace multiple disciplinary orientations to writing instruction. At the same time, writing should be an integrated practice of learning and inquiry within all disciplines. And, it should be practiced in multiple environments (from classrooms to labs to fields to homes) using multiple applications (from pencil to web-based programs).
Why	The study and practice of writing should enable students to compose for different purposes and audiences across a variety of genres and contexts in order to achieve specified goals. It should prepare students for success in school, home, and work. It should increase critical thinking skills and deepen learning of content. And it should provide students with the ability to be active, critical citizens in a changing world.

Figure 3.2. What Really Matters in Teaching Writing

Using a very different research method than those above, researchers commissioned by Carnegie Corporation reached similar conclusions in identifying effective writing instruction for 4th–12th grade students. Through a statistical meta-analysis of 133 experimental or quasi-experimental studies, Steve Graham and Dolores Perin were able to identify the eleven most effective approaches to improving student writing in importance of effect from highest to lowest:

1. Writing Strategies, which involves teaching students strategies for planning, revising, and editing their compositions
2. Summarization, which involves explicitly and systematically teaching students how to summarize texts

3. Collaborative Writing, which uses instructional arrangements in which adolescents work together to plan, draft, revise, and edit their compositions

4. Specific Product Goals, which assigns students specific, reachable goals for the writing they are to complete

5. Word Processing, which uses computers and word processors as instructional supports for writing assignments

6. Sentence Combining, which involves teaching students to construct more complex, sophisticated sentences

7. Prewriting, which engages students in activities designed to help them generate or organize ideas for their composition

8. Inquiry Activities, which engages students in analyzing immediate, concrete data to help them develop ideas and content for a particular writing task

9. Process Writing Approach, which interweaves a number of writing instructional activities in a workshop environment that stresses extended writing opportunities, writing for authentic audiences, personalized instruction, and cycles of writing

10. Study of Models, which provides students with opportunities to read, analyze, and emulate models of good writing

11. Writing for Content Learning, which uses writing as a tool for learning content material ("Writing Next: Effective Strategies to Improve Writing of Adolescents in Middle and High Schools")

If we turn our attention to research on college readiness, we will again see substantial overlap in research-based best practices. For example, if we incorporate the "Framework for Success in Postsecondary Writing," developed by the Council of Writing Program Administrators, National Council of Teachers of English, and National Writing Project, we find that current research on writing and the teaching of writing emphasizes:

- Developing Rhetorical Knowledge—or the ability to adapt to compose for different purposes, audiences, and context across a variety of texts, disciplines, and settings

- Developing Critical Thinking Through Writing, Reading, and Research—or the ability to analyze situations and texts on a variety of levels as well as exhibit multiple ways of understanding situations and texts

- Developing Flexible Writing Processes—or the ability to employ a variety of writing tools and strategies during the development of a final product such as generating ideas, incorporating evidence from multiple sources, employing effective revision work, and possessing a meta-awareness of their own development as a writer

- Developing Knowledge Conventions—or the ability to correctly use the formal and informal guidelines that govern different types of texts (e.g., knowing how and why texts such as lab reports and autobiographies differ as well as being able to compose these different genres)

- Composing in Multiple Environments—or the ability to write using a variety of technologies (from a pencil to a web-based computer application) and to understand how the use of various technologies affect reading and writing practices (6–10)

A synthesis of these results (Figure 3.2) makes clear what matters in the teaching of writing.

It is vitally important that these best practices not be taught in isolation, but rather as part of a larger vertical effort across disciplines and a horizontal effort through grades. To this end, Chapter Four emphasizes *transfer* as both a method and methodology for supporting best practices in vertical and horizontal curricula that can lead to improved writing instruction. Finally, these widely agreed upon best practices are only as good as the structures we build to enact and energize them. In the next section we touch briefly on matters of professional development, and offer one example of how professional development, standardized tests, effective instruction, and writing across the curriculum come together. In our final chapter we focus in-depth on the role of professional development in positioning teachers as sponsors of literacy, enabled to intervene in meaningful ways in shaping the future.

PROFESSIONAL DEVELOPMENT AND ASSESSMENT

To talk about writing across the curriculum and effective and responsive instruction is relatively meaningless without support for the ongoing professional development of our teachers and administrators. As teachers at any level can attest, the often-stated advice to "adopt best practices" is seldom followed by the types of support needed for the sustained adoption of best practices over time. Simply attending a conference or workshop or working on an isolated level to make one's own classroom a site for best practices does not create the kinds of ongoing opportunities for growth and change required. The urgency with which many express the need for sustainable professional development is clear in the summary of the consensus reached among teachers, administrators, researchers, and other education officials who participated in the National Commission on Writing hearings:

> Scarcely an hour went by at any of the hearings without a strong plea to strengthen programs to help teachers improve writing instruction. Recommendations in this area began with the suggestion that districts transform professional development by turning the responsibility and funding for it over to teachers. The sense was that professional development led by teachers can support and empower them, while grounding professional development in challenges that are immediate and relevant in the classroom. There was also a hope that teacher-led professional development emphasizing teachers as writers could show teachers how to model writing for their students and allow teachers to understand the challenges that students experience learning to write. Encouraging teachers to see themselves as writers and modeling writing for the benefit of their students were recurring themes throughout the hearings. (*Writing and School Reform* 26)

Another strong theme to emerge in relation to professional development was the importance of mentoring. In particular, participants emphasized expanded university-school partnerships that allowed for joint defining and sharing of best practices and reversing teacher turnover rates (26).

Assessment activities, even standardized tests of writing, can be used to support effective writing across the curriculum instruction through professional development. As an example we can look at the work of the Council of Independent Colleges/Collegiate Learning Assessment Consortium, which in 2011 published "Catalyst for Change: CIC/CLA Consortium." From fall 2008 until spring 2011, forty-seven colleges and universities administered the CLA on their campuses, working as a group to determine the most effective ways to improve instruction through assessment. The CLA results were triangulated with other measures, measures differing by campus in order to meet the challenges of each unique context. Interestingly, this report does not focus on gains in student achievement over the research period, likely because it is not a long enough time period to achieve substantial gains. What the report does focus on is the change in instructional activities, including writing across the curriculum and assessment, as well as sustainable professional development opportunities generated through participation in the consortium (itself a long-term opportunity to identify and adopt best practices through professional development). Weaving together excerpts from this report shows a repetition of some of the main themes we have been highlighting, including the fact that too many of our claims have been based on anecdotal evidence and fuzzy admonitions instead of empirical analysis. Further, this report again shows that the establishment of professional communities of practice, not unfunded mandates for standardized tests of accountability, are essential to any educational reform movement:

> . . . [W]hen the Council for Aid to Education (CAE) first asked the Council of Independent Colleges (CIC) to help select a few colleges to participate in a pilot project that would measure the effects of an institution on how much the students had learned during college, CIC jumped at the opportunity. It had been our view that the prevailing and largely anecdotal ways of describing the distinctive educational advantages of smaller, largely residential, liberal arts-based, private colleges and universities had been only modestly persuasive and a more empirical approach was needed. (2)
>
> . . . [T]he CIC/CLA Consortium established a professional community of practice that supports common measures and practices in assessing and improving student learning. For many years, a common phrase and injunction in efforts to improve higher education has been the need to adopt "best practices." However, the movement from going to a conference or workshop in which an interesting "best practice" is discussed to going back to campus and putting it into practice is usually problematic. Getting attention for an idea can be challenging, let alone acquiring the time and efforts of individuals actually needed to experiment with a new initiative. (42)

> The CIC/CLA Consortium experience provides two ways to bridge the gap between a best practice, on the one hand, and innovation and campus implementation, on the other. First, providing a common measure across a set of similar institutions gives it some measure of credibility. In the case of the CLA, apart from its intuitive validity, the very fact that a number of institutions were committing to experiment with this instrument gave the work some initial legitimacy and traction. Second, the existence of ongoing meetings of the consortium provided a real opportunity for "best practices"

to be developed and disseminated. Repeatedly, consortium colleges and universities commented on how interactions with other institutions provided advice on everything from logistical challenges of testing students to the broadest ideas about curriculum and program. The work of the CIC/CLA Consortium provides a model of how undergraduate education can become more professionalized through shared understandings, measures, and practices. (42–43)

In describing the increased emphasis on writing across the curriculum, the report focuses on the widespread use of concepts that led to an increased use of engaging performance-based tasks, such as the development of a referendum on cell phone use while driving in a psychology class and a debate team event focusing on molecules of emotion (mind/body connections), and a team-taught interdisciplinary chemistry and psychology course that included a lab on mind/body interconnectedness (29). What is most important here is that these changes were not a result of strictly defined standards and rubrics being imposed on learning communities based on the results of standardized test. Rather, as the authors of this report make clear:

What is particularly valuable about the consortium in this regard is that it is perfectly consistent with the traditional autonomy and diversity of colleges and universities. The scope and variety of the work of these institutions coupled with the interaction through the consortium offers the possibility for continuing experimentation and imitation. Because these are independent institutions, they can readily adopt best practices as they see them and adapt them to fit their individual circumstances. The community of professional practice represented by the consortium shows how greater consistency, attention to evidence, transparency, and, ultimately, improvement is consistent with institutional autonomy and diversity. (42–43)

We'd like to point out here that the value of "performance tasks" might not be considered revelatory given all of the research cited in the previous sections of this chapter—much of which explicitly supports the use of these types of writing assignments across the curriculum. What is important here is not so much that participants reached this conclusion, but rather that through ongoing professional development informed by assessment, these schools were able to build a sustainable structure for change that is responsive to evolving student needs.

ONE LAST POINT—LET'S NOT FORGET
ENGLISH LANGUAGE LEARNERS

While it is outside the scope of this book to give adequate attention to how we might address the issues raised here from the perspective of English language learners (ELL), it is a topic of too much importance for us not to raise it at all. A number of the studies and research reports we have been synthesizing do make mention of English language learners. English language learners are generally considered the fastest growing population in our public schools, and participants in *Writing Reform Now* hearings "stressed the importance of responding to the special needs of English language learners in assessment. Practically all teachers require support, assistance, and professional development to help these students succeed in both their native language and English (27). However, at the time of this writing, thirty-four states have received waivers from the requirements of NCLB. And, while we are not fans of NCLB, we are concerned that these waivers may lead to a lack of focus and support for English language learners. The American Institutes for Research (AIR) points out that the plans submitted by states are largely lacking in attention to ELLs, despite their ever-increasing numbers in our classrooms and the wide and persistent gap between ELLs and English-proficient students evidenced in the latest results of the National Assessment of Educational Progress. In an effort to provide guidance to states with waivers, the American Institutes for Research has taken up the call to make sure the needs of second language learners are being met. Its guide, "Supporting English Language Learners: A Pocket Guide for State and District Leaders" focuses specifically on ensuring that English language learners have the support needed to become college and/or career ready through effective instruction and leadership.

CHAPTER 4

THINKING VERTICALLY

As we argue in Chapter Three and in this chapter, there is significant agreement among a variety of stakeholders concerning just what it is that we should be doing in our writing classrooms in order to prepare students for lifelong success as literate actors in the world. There is also significant agreement about the macro-level, high-impact practices shown to improve student learning. How, then, might we chart a path forward that takes into account the many complexities we've discussed throughout this book? Relatedly, how might we quickly and effectively intervene in current efforts to shape writing instruction at the high school and college level? We will now focus on the moments of opportunity presented to us through debates surrounding the Common Core State Standards. In particular, we propose acting at the confluence of Core to College driven initiatives, research on transfer emerging within rhetorical genre studies, and an investment in K–College professional learning communities at the local and national level. In short, we advocate for First-Year Composition curricular development projects, vertically aligned with high school curricula, as well as writing across the curriculum at all levels, that teachers, researchers, and state policymakers can all endorse. Along the way, we must reassert the agency of teachers and students as we recreate assessment not as a tool of accountability, but rather a teaching and learning practice rooted in context-driven standards.

COMMON CORE STATE STANDARDS INITIATIVE

Let's begin by taking time to more fully understand the Common Core State Standards in general, and the Language Arts/Writing Across the Curriculum strands in particular, in order to have a better sense of how we might leverage them in debates about literacy instruction at the college level. The Common Core State Standards are intended to provide a common set of milestones for grades K–12; skills are to build from year to year, so that current learning scaffolds upon prior knowledge and skills. The Common Core State Standards Initiative claims that the standards:

- Are aligned with college and work expectations;
- Are clear, understandable and consistent;
- Include rigorous content and application of knowledge through high-order skills;

- Build upon strengths and lessons of current state standards;
- Are informed by other top performing countries, so that all students are prepared to succeed in our global economy and society; and
- Are evidence-based. ("About the Standards")

Previous attempts at standards-based education varied by state, causing a problem for curriculum development and textbook selection. As John Kendall claims, "Standards were out in front, while curriculum to support these standards lagged behind. This lag crippled districts' and schools' attempts to implement standards-based instruction and has been counted by many as the single greatest failing of the standards movement" (6). Furthermore, having local state-by-state standards but an increasingly transient population meant that as new students relocate into a school district, teachers have no easy way of knowing what prior knowledge the students are bringing with them.

The CCSS, which include detailed discussions of goals for each level and suggested curricular content as well as a rising tide of attendant professional development networks, intend to provide national standards that will make previous issues of curriculum support, textbook development, and student mobility less problematic. In addition, these standards are focused not just at the high school level, as some state standards initiatives are; rather, they encompass a student's entire school experience from kindergarten through 12th grade and into college (e.g., Core to College). The comprehensiveness of the Common Core is important for those of us in higher education to understand. Because Core to College initiatives are already in place, universities might experience the results of the CCSS on student learning relatively soon.

As writing teachers and researchers, we are supportive of the intent of the CCSS. In particular, we are emboldened by the emphasis on literacy (reading, writing, speaking, and listening) as a shared responsibility across grade levels and content areas, as well as the increased expectations for the variety and complexity of the texts students read and write across the curriculum—especially nonfiction texts. And we are encouraged by the efforts to create partnerships among K–12 and college teachers. Still, given the history of writing instruction and standardized testing in the United States, we also have serious concerns.

Much like the earlier rhetoric of crisis following Sputnik that led to the National Assessment of Educational Progress, as detailed in Chapter One, the CCSS are being propelled by a fear that the United States is falling dangerously behind other countries in global tests of academic achievement. More specifically, as the October 7, 2013, issue of *Time* magazine proclaimed: "What's driving the core standards conversation now is the ambition to succeed in a global economy and the anxiety that American students are failing to do so" (Meacham

44). But a critical difference is that in the case of the National Assessment of Educational Progress, the federal government was the main driver and investor. In the case of the CCSS, the federal government seems to be trying to appear as little more than a supportive bystander in an effort seemingly driven by states, but really fueled by private foundations and testing companies. As explained by Thomas Newkirk in "Speaking Back to the Common Core":

> A number of literacy educators have chosen to cherry-pick—
> endorse the standards but not the tests; yet they are clearly a
> package. The Department of Education has committed 300
> million dollars to the creation of these new tests, which are
> now being designed by two consortia, PARCC and Smarter
> Balanced. These tests will give operational reality to the stan-
> dards—in effect they will become the standards; there will be
> little incentive to teach to skills that are not tested (this is a
> lesson from No Child Left Behind). (4)

The Smarter Balanced Testing Consortium and the Partnership for Readiness for College and Careers (PARCC) were among the first to develop and offer comprehensive systems to measure student mastery of CCSS. We have been focusing on PARCC simply because we both live and work in PARCC member states and so are more familiar with its history and trajectory. We are concerned not only with the continued narrowing of the curriculum and the lack of student and teacher agency such a well-funded system of accountability entails, we are also concerned that some states have already committed to using the results of the PARCC assessments given in high school for college placement and admission decisions ("Colorado Measures of Academic Success"; Illinois State Board of Education "PARCC Assessment FAQs"). Further, the lack of diversity in our assessment practices that such concentration on a single measure of student achievement will result in is likely to limit access to many students who, as William Hiss and Valerie Franks show us in their study on test-optional colleges and universities, "have proven themselves to everyone but the testing agencies" (61).

Research has begun to emerge on the effects of CCSS. While some argue it is too early to measure the effects of our latest educational reform project, many states are considered early and strong adopters of CCSS, aiming for full implementation in 2012–2013 (Loveless), and it is reasonable to use these states as a starting point. In fact, some states are already in their fifth year of implementation. This is not to say that we believe all students and teachers have been provided with the support structures needed to meet these new standards, but rather that we have much to learn by working to understand whether or not CCSS is evidencing its intended effects earlier rather than later. Further, briefly revisiting the outcomes of No Child Left Behind over the decade of its strongest implementation period provides us with a way of benchmarking Common Core State Standards.

NCLB required states to test students every year in grades 3 through 8 and once in high school to determine whether or not schools were meeting "Adequate Yearly Progress" as defined by NCLB. The National Assessment of Educational Progress (NAEP) was designated as a test of achievement that would be independent of the state-controlled tests. While the law authorizing NCLB was signed in 2001, it is generally agreed upon that it did not take effect until 2003. In 2012, the National Center for Fair and Open Testing published "NCLB's Lost Decade for Educational Progress: What Can We Learn from this Policy Failure?" As this report, and many others conclude:

> Overall, growth on NAEP was more rapid before NCLB
> became law and flattened after it took effect. For example, 4th
> grade math scores jumped 11 points between 1996 and 2003,
> but increased only 6 points between 2003 and 2011. Reading
> scores have barely moved in the post-NCLB era. Fourth grade
> scores increased just 3 points to 221 between 2003 and 2011,
> remaining level since 2007. In 8th grade reading, there was a
> meager 2-point increase, from 263 to 265, in that same pe-
> riod. Since the start of NCLB, gains have stagnated or slowed
> for almost every demographic group in both subjects and
> both grades. (Guisbond with Neill and Schaeffer 3)

These results suggest that not only has NCLB failed to result in the intended increase in student achievement as measured by the independent NAEP, but the only modest gains occurred very early in the process, as is often the case when adopting innovations of any type. It will be important to see if CCSS follows a similar trend.

There is certainly considerable variation in the timing and strength of individual states' adoption of CCSS that should be taken into account when assessing early results of the CCSS initiative. Tom Loveless, in "Measuring Effects of the Common Core," uses two indexes to categorize states as strong adopters, medium adopters, and non-adopters. The 2011 index lists nineteen states as strong adopters, twenty-seven as medium adopters, and four as non-adopters. Strong adopters spent considerably more money on CCSS and engaged in at least three implementation strategies—professional development, new instructional material, and participation in one of two testing consortia (PARCC or SBAC). Medium adopters engaged in at least two of the three implementation strategies listed above. Non-adopters did not adopt the CCSS at all. The 2013 index is based on each state's timeline for classroom implementation of CCSS, with twelve states listing 2012–2013 as their implementation date and thus categorized as strong adopters, thirty-four states identifying an implementation date after 2012–2013 and thus categorized as medium adopters, and four states as non-adopters. Based on these indexes, Loveless examined 2009–2013 NAEP scores:

> Fourth grade reading scores improved by 1.11 scale score points in states with strong implementation of CCSS compared to states that did not adopt CCSS. A similar comparison in last year's BCR [Brown Center Report] found a 1.27 point difference on NAEP's eighth grade math test, also in favor of states with strong implementation of CCSS. These differences, although certainly encouraging to CCSS supporters, are quite small, amounting to (at most) 0.04 standard deviations (SD) on the NAEP scale. A threshold of 0.20 SD—five times larger—is often invoked as the minimum size for a test score change to be regarded as noticeable.

Because the NAEP writing test was last administered in 2011 and is not scheduled to be administered again until 2017, we are not in a position to say much about CCSS in relation to writing and NAEP assessments.

Of course, it remains to be seen, as was the case with early results from NCLB, if this is as high as the gains will be over time. There is some additional evidence that this may be the case. For example, a series of reports was prepared for the National Center for Educational Statistics (overseers of NAEP) on the degree of alignment between NAEP and CCSS by the American Institutes of Research. Among the findings for K–8 math are that there were not significant areas of content in the NAEP mathematics framework that are not also in the CCSS math standards. However, there are some important differences to note: the algebra and geometry content in the CCSS math standards are more rigorous than in the NAEP framework; certain skills, such as the ability to estimate, are woven throughout the CCSS math standards but assessed in isolation in the NAEP; conceptual understanding of a greater number of math topics is required by the CCSS math standards; and certain math content is introduced at a higher grade level in the CCSS math standards (Hughes et al. 11). Given this raising of the bar in the CCSS math standards, it's interesting that states categorized as strong adopters of CCSS didn't show stronger gains in math on the NAEP assessments.

In a parallel validity study for the National Center of Education Statistics on reading and writing, led by Karen Wixson et al. of the American Institutes of Research, we can see how the CCSS ELA standards align with the NAEP reading and writing assessments. The authors found that many elements of the NAEP reading assessment are in line with current research and the CCSS-ELA standards. Further, the reading selections for grades four and eight are within or above the ranges specified in the CCSS-ELA, while the grade twelve passages are below the ranges specified in the CCSS-ELA (92). Importantly, "Panel members caution NAEP to be cognizant of the lack of research base, inconsistencies, and specificity of the 'learning progressions' embodied by the K–12 grade-level standards in CCSS-ELA" (93).

As with reading, the panel found that the NAEP writing assessment reflects current research on writing and major elements of the CCSS-ELA standards, with both emphasizing writing as a social act. Importance is placed on the role of audience, purpose, task, and rhetorical knowledge as well as the development of ideas, organization, and language facility and conventions (94). Beyond these similarities, the panel points out that the CCSS-ELA emphasizes writing from sources and performance-based tasks while the NAEP assessment relies on writing from background knowledge and personal experience (95). CCSS-ELA also places emphasis on writing in the disciplines, including the use of domain-specific vocabulary (95) as part of an overall shift toward non-fiction texts in ELA classrooms.

Indeed, some consider the shift away from a near exclusive focus on fictional texts in English Language Arts classrooms toward a balance of fiction and non-fiction text to be among the most controversial shifts CCSS recommend. Here the NAEP can also be helpful as it asks questions of teachers about their professional development activities and instructional practices. As reported by Loveless in "Measuring Effects of the Common Core,": "Fourth grade teachers in strong implementation states decisively favored the use of fiction over nonfiction in 2009 and 2011. But the prominence of fiction in those states experienced a large decline in 2013 (-12.4 percentage points). The decline for the entire four year period, 2009–2013, was larger in the strong implementation states (-10.8) than in the medium implementation (-7.5) or non-adoption states (-9.8)." This data suggests that even if adoption of CCSS does not lead to dramatically improved reading and writing scores on standardized tests, it can lead to a significant improvement in certain widely agreed upon recommendations about best practices in writing instruction, including that students read and write in a variety of genres across disciplines and that these genres move beyond traditionally defined academic writing. Taking a closer look at the Language and Literacy Common Core State Standards will show why this is the case.

LANGUAGE AND LITERACY COMMON CORE STATE STANDARDS

The English Language Arts standards for K–12 are divided into four strands. The reading and writing strands have ten standards each while the speaking/listening and language strands have six standards each. So many standards could be difficult to cover during the year in a meaningful way for student learning. However, unlike many other state-based standards, the Common Core seems to strike a workable integration of language and literacy standards within the context of other disciplines. In fact, Common Core Standards for English Language Arts and Literacy in History/Social Studies, Science and Technical subjects states:

> Just as students must learn to read, write, speak, listen, and use language effectively in a variety of content areas, so too must the Standards specify the literacy skills and understandings required for college and career readiness in multiple disciplines. Literacy standards for grade 6 and above are predicated on teachers of ELA, history/social studies, science, and technical subjects using their content area expertise to help students meet the particular challenges of reading, writing, speaking, listening, and language in their respective fields. It is important to note that the 6–12 literacy standards in history/social studies, science, and technical subjects are not meant to replace content standards in those areas but rather to supplement them.

The four strands of the language and literacy standards (reading, speaking and listening, language, and writing) create "a set of College and Career Readiness (CCR) Anchor Standards that broadly describe what students should be able to do, from kindergarten through 12th grade" (Kendall 12–13) in order to be prepared for higher education and/or work. Certainly, there is overlap between these strands. Language, which is concerned primarily with vocabulary, is important for writing and reading. Likewise, speaking and listening, which has as one of its concerns presenting ideas to an audience, overlaps with written rhetoric's focus on audience-based writing. As most readers of this book rightly understand, there is a deep interconnectedness between reading, writing, speaking/listening, and language use.

In terms of the writing strand, the Common Core Standards focus on three "text types and purposes": arguments, informative/explanatory texts, and narratives (Common Core ELA Standards 18). Other standards in this strand focus on appropriate development and organization for audience and purpose; the writing process; the use of technology for production of, collaboration on, or dissemination of writing; research skills to find and evaluate credible sources from a variety of media; academic honesty when using sources; the use of analysis and close reading as evidence; and writing in both shorter and longer time frames for varying audiences and purposes (18). We note significant alignment of the Common Core with Graham and Perin's eleven most effective approaches to improving student writing, as discussed in Chapter Three.

As Kendall posits, one of the strengths of the Common Core writing standards is the focus on argument, which many state standards did not have. He notes that states did have "persuasion" as a type of writing, "but in a form that appeals to the audience through emotions or the character or credentials of the writer rather than depending upon argument, which seeks to convince the audience by means of the perceived merit of the claims and proof offered" (18). Wolfe's analysis of assignments across myriad disciplines, on the other hand, indicates that argumentation is one of the primary genres used. Therefore, the Common Core's emphasis on argumentation rather than persuasion supports college-ready writers.

We appreciate the intent of the Common Core State Standards to bring consistent standards across states, to prepare students for college or for the demands of a twenty-first century workforce that continues to demand more of workers, to emphasize writing and literacy in broad ways, across genres and disciplines, and to establish rigorous achievement levels for students. We further think that the notion of knowledge scaffolding on which the Common Core State Standards were built is cognitively and pedagogically sound. We are also encouraged by how all of this might bring K–12 and college faculty together. At the same time, we are very much concerned with how the CCSS are being positioned, not simply to prepare students for college, but perhaps also to drive the college curriculum itself. Still, like Thomas Newkirk, we are hopeful skeptics:

> It may be that the CCSS does what others claim they will—
> encourage good pedagogical discussion, clarify goals, help
> students read deeply, give writing its proper place in the
> curriculum, expand the repertoire in English Language Arts
> to a focus on quality nonfiction. And that the initiative won't
> dissolve into teaching new tests. (6)

If the Common Core is not co-opted by the assessment industrial complex, and continues to promote a meaningful partnership between K–12 and college faculty, we see value in CCSS in the long term as the overall framework for CCSS supports existing and emerging research in best practices for writing instruction across the curriculum. In the rest of this chapter, we highlight the areas of most promise that should not only guide that ongoing implementation of CCSS, but also our work at the university level.

KNOWLEDGE TRANSFER

Recently, writing studies has seen a reemergence of interest in cognitive-based research—in particular, the notion of knowledge transfer has become the subject of theoretical discussion and empirical investigation. D.N Perkins and Gavriel Salomon in their seminal article "Teaching for Transfer" define transfer as "knowledge or skill associated with one context that reaches out to enhance another. Transfer goes beyond ordinary learning in that the skill or knowledge in question has to travel to a new context" (22). Knowledge transfer can occur both inside and outside of educational settings. Most educators believe that transfer is important and that it needs to happen in order for students to move fluidly from one context to another where they adapt and apply prior knowledge. Yet, as Perkins and Salomon suggest, most teachers believe that transfer will "take care of itself," what they call the "Bo Peep Theory": If left alone, the sheep will find Bo Peep" (23). Gerald Nelms and Ronda Dively distinguish the difference between "learning" and "transfer." Drawing upon many sources, they define learning as "the durability of knowledge—that is information stored in memory" whereas transfer "involves the application of knowledge acquired in one situation or context to a different situation or context." They continue: "Of course, learning is a crucial prerequisite for transfer," but argue that unless transfer occurs, education is not successful (215).

Transfer, however, is not easily achieved, and Perkins and Salomon posit that transfer may be difficult to achieve because of several factors—either the knowledge needed is not deeply enough learned so that it can be transferred, or it may not be able to be applied to various contexts because it has not been "cognitively assimilated." It could be, they argue, that knowledge is so closely tied to its locus and to specialized knowledge that it cannot be transferred to other contexts, what they call "local knowledge" (24). Offering the "low road and high road model" of transfer, Perkins and Salomon suggest ways transfer might be successful. Low road transfer, they suggest, occurs when significant overlap exists between prior knowledge and a current situation. They suggest that one could drive a truck based on prior knowledge of how to drive a car (25). In other words, between these two contexts, significant overlap exists. High road transfer, on the other hand, relies "on deliberate mindful abstraction of skill or knowledge from one context for application to another" (25). Two kinds of high road transfer exist: "forward reaching and backward reaching" (26). "In forward-reaching high road transfer, one learns something and abstracts it in preparation for application elsewhere" while in backward reaching transfer "one finds oneself in a problem situation, abstracts key characteristics from the situation and reaches backward into one's experiences for matches" (26). Low road transfer, Perkins and Salomon suggest, is the easiest way for transfer to occur, while high road transfer is more difficult, but not impossible, to attain. They argue that in order for transfer to occur, students must be explicitly taught about transfer at a meta-cognitive level: "Accordingly, a major goal of teaching for transfer becomes not just teaching particular knowledge and skills for transfer but teaching students in general how to *learn for transfer*" (30).

Although Perkins and Salomon provide an often-used framework for understanding transfer, theirs is not the only one to consider. Indeed, researchers in writing studies have begun to refine notions of transfer within the context of what we already know about literacy development. For example, Elizabeth Wardle discusses three understandings of transfer: (1) "'Task' Conceptions," which resemble Perkins and Salomon's understanding of transfer and "theorize transfer as a transition of knowledge used in one task to solve another task" ("Understanding Transfer" 68); (2) "'Individual' Conceptions," which focuses on "teach[ing] students 'learned intelligent behavior' that will help them seek out and/or create situations in which what they have learned will transfer" (67); and (3) "'Context' Conceptions," which go beyond the task or the individual to the larger social context, whether it be "situated," "sociocultural," or "activity-based" (67–68). Wardle suggests that activity-based transfer may help us think more broadly about transfer:

> [A]ccording to the complex understandings of transfer that
> emerge from activity-based theories, some previously learned
> knowledge and skills that are appropriate for and needed in a
> new context or activity system may be applied differently than
> in the context or activity system in which they were learned.
> Therefore, if we look, but do not find direct evidence that
> students use specific previously learned skills in new situations,
> we cannot necessarily assume that students did not learn them,
> have not used them, or will not use them in the future. (69)

Positioned more concretely, we might envision transfer as a problem-solving negotiation that writers enter into upon experiencing a new context. The question then becomes less about the student's prior knowledge of various genres and more about the student's meta-awareness of problem-solving strategies as literate actors in the world. Thinking about transfer is important since first-year writing courses are often key components to general education requirements at most colleges and universities. The assumption is and has been that what students learn in first-year writing courses can be transferred to other writing situations throughout their university experience and even into the workplace, although David Smit has argued this is likely an erroneous assumption on our part. Several recent empirical studies have attempted to determine whether or not transfer is occurring from first-year writing to the other writing tasks that students face in the university. Results of these studies suggest that two central themes occur: Transfer and genre are linked, and transfer is also connected to behaviors and meta-awareness.

TRANSFER AND GENRES

First-year writing programs generally predicate their value upon the assumptions that students are prepared to write beyond the typical two required courses, that students are taught writing strategies and behaviors such as drafting and revising that supersede any specific type of writing, and that students who have had little experience writing more than a five-paragraph essay will broaden their abilities to write longer, sustained pieces often involving research. These are noble goals. The reality, however, is that writing courses are often relegated to graduate students, adjuncts, or tenure-track faculty who may not be prepared for or interested in teaching writing. Often these faculty value and teach their students to replicate the kinds of writing done in literature to the exclusion of other disciplines in the liberal arts, let alone the "hard" sciences. And, seldom does this teaching include the vertical transfer of skills that might allow us to argue that those literary skills do, indeed, have value outside of English.

The results of Wardle's 2009 study suggest as much. While Wardle noted that the genres assigned are diverse, there are genres that are assigned beyond composition, such as an observation and an argument. However, Wardle suggests that the way these assignments are structured for a composition course—and the way in which the rhetorical situation is constructed—make the assignments less transferrable and more unique to first year composition "genres" than to disciplinary genres, what she calls "mutt genres." "They are asked to write mutt genres," Wardle argues, "because the exigencies giving rise to the genre in other courses are not available within FYC (nor can they be expected to be available). Thus, FYC students are told to write an argument . . . simply for the sake of doing so (i.e., for 'practice')" (777). The lack of consistent genre instruction may be a factor in students' ability to transfer knowledge from first-year writing courses.

Similarly, Linda Bergmann and Janet Zepernick's research, conducted at an engineering-focused school—which admittedly could affect their results—suggests that students separate writing done in English courses from the writing done in disciplinary content courses. Writing done in disciplinary courses is part of "their socialization into the disciplines" (129). Furthermore students view the personal writing assigned in composition courses as not rule-governed and idiosyncratic. In their disciplinary writing, however, students indicated that they understood the disciplinary boundaries and expectations for their writing. For that reason, students reported that while they generally thought writing skills are transferrable, they did not believe that the skills they learned in first-year writing courses were transferrable since they were not disciplinary in orientation (129).

In their cross-institutional study, Mary Jo Reiff and Anis Bawarshi asked participants to acknowledge the kinds of writing tasks they had performed prior to matriculating at their respective universities. Students at the University of Tennessee overwhelmingly reported the research paper as their top genre, while the five-paragraph essay was the predominant genre reported by University of Washington students (321). Beyond academic writing, students reported writing in their personal lives as well, including emails, text messages, and business letters, results that are quite similar to those noted by the WIDE Research Group at Michigan State University's cross-institutional study. Interestingly, when asked to reflect upon the genre knowledge they utilized when approaching a specific writing task in FYC, "students tended not to report drawing upon the full range of their genre knowledge" (323). They would not necessarily, for example, draw upon their out-of-school genre knowledge for an academic assignment; even if such prior knowledge might have been seen as relevant by the researchers, it was not by the students (324).

Across these studies, we can begin to see how situatedness in genre may prove to be critical to a student's ability to transfer knowledge from one writing situation to another. We must be careful, however, not to assume that more exposure to a wide array of genres is the key to transfer. In other words, we cannot necessarily jump to the conclusion that teaching all genres will lead to transfer. It could lead to learning, perhaps, but not transfer if we think of transfer as the ability to apply knowledge from one situation or social context to another. Teaching all genres would also be impossible in a composition classroom as well, leading to the mutt genres divorced of rhetorical exigency that Wardle described. Amy Devitt argues that genre knowledge is not transferrable since "they do not meet the needs of the [new] situation fully" (222). Antecedent genres, which Devitt defines as "the known genres that writers use in new situations" (221–22) provide writers with a foundation upon which to approach a new writing task in a new genre. Writers develop awareness of their antecedent genres though meta-awareness about writing, and this meta-awareness does seem to be something that students can learn in first-year writing and transfer beyond. Further, in support of CCSS insistence on reading and writing across the disciplines, including a significant shift toward a balanced approach in English Language Arts when it comes to increased emphasis on nonfiction in English Language Arts classrooms, we find significant opportunity to leverage CCSS in teaching toward transfer.

For example, every three to five years the ACT National Curriculum Survey asks teachers in high school and college what they teach as well as what they think about the most pressing educational issues of the day. The most recent survey was conducted in 2012. This survey revealed that while high school literature and reading teachers "place a good deal of importance on topics requiring knowledge of content such as literary techniques and devices, literary genres and subgenres, and literary history and periods" this type of content knowledge is considered much less important by those who teach first-year college literature courses (5). We would add that it is even less important to those of us who teach first-year composition courses. This focus on content knowledge represents a misalignment between high school preparation and college expectations. If we shift our focus to center on transfer, high school literature and reading courses would include literary nonfiction, teaching students how to use literary techniques to document, synthesize, and argue real-world issues. In this way, we are not suggesting abandonment of literary study, but rather agreeing with the recommendation of ACT:

> Rather than eliminate the analytical techniques inherent to the study of literary content knowledge in high school, high school teachers could bring these techniques to bear on a wider range of texts important to a variety of disciplines and careers, fostering critical engagement and highlighting the broad importance of reading comprehension skills in general . . . [while] emphasiz[ing] the creative component inherent in persuasive and informational writing, while still exposing students to the expressive benefits of learning to write fiction and poetry." (10)

BEHAVIORS AND META-AWARENESS

While the students in Wardle's study self-reported that they gained new knowledge about writing in their first-year composition class, such as strategies for approaching and managing research-based writing or new rhetorical approaches to organization, and that they gained meta-awareness of language use across various contexts, they claimed that they did not have to use these strategies in order to be successful in writing in their disciplinary courses. Her analysis of other data suggests that when students participated in "engaging and challenging writing assignments" they were able to occasionally transfer knowledge, "but rarely consciously" (79). Bergmann and Zepernick suggest that students do not seek ways they can apply the skills learned in FYC to other writing tasks (139). Both

Wardle's and Bergmann and Zepernick's studies provide evidence that what students learn may not be raised to their consciousness as they move out of FYC and into disciplinary intensive courses. Nor are they, as Wardle notes, able to articulate that meta-awareness.

Drawing upon Nancy Sommers and Laura Saltz's notion of boundary crossers, Reiff and Bawarshi's results suggest that apart from confidence, one indicator of a student's likelihood of being a boundary crosser—that is someone who is able to engage in high-road transfer—is the ability to move from "reliance upon whole genres to reliance upon smaller constellations of strategies" (326). Successful writers in their study were able to go beyond noting that a new writing task resembled an antecedent genre to use Devitt's term, but rather to begin examining various prior strategies that they had used. Boundary guarders—those who utilize low-road transfer of prior genre knowledge, holding close to their prior knowledge—rely upon whole genres rather than strategies. It would seem, then, that when students are able to gain perspective and distance at the meta-level, they are able to deconstruct what they know and reassemble it as needed to approach other writing tasks.

TEACHING VERTICALLY

Given the rather ominous tone in many sections of this book, we want to offer hope to readers that all is not lost. In fact, we think the intersection of CCSS and knowledge transfer can lead us to think about how we should be addressing genre knowledge from the earliest beginnings of writing, and how we should begin to re-shape what it is that we are doing. We also want to be very clear that we are not suggesting that the proverbial baby be thrown out with the bathwater. We firmly believe that required writing courses play an integral role in students' college curriculum—and perhaps even more so today than ever before. We also do not intend to suggest that disciplinary study or humanistic inquiry be shortchanged, or to suggest that first-year writing exist purely to offer support to professional schools (an issue that is close to both of our hearts as our campuses increasingly favor professional schools). As many colleges and universities are reducing the hours required for graduation to improve student retention and time to graduation (two metrics that are tied to state funding for higher education in Illinois and Colorado, for example) and to reduce students' potential student loan debt (an issue of significance for the financial health of students and our country), having a required sequence will be essential for students. Indeed, the NCTE Research Policy Brief "First Year Writing: What Good Does it Do?" confirms first-year writing courses improve student engagement and retention as well as develop students' rhetorical knowledge, metacognition, and sense of responsibility. Given the possible potential threat to reducing composition courses as hours are being redistributed, we need to make sure these courses are doing the very best job for our students in the few weeks we have with them to promote their successful growth as writers in their future coursework and in their future employment.

What might such a curriculum look like? As we have hinted with the title of this chapter, we argue for a vertical writing pedagogy that leverages the best intents of the CCSS and knowledge transfer. Building upon the knowledge that students will have learned under CCSS, which is a vertical model that builds in developmentally appropriate ways from one year of schooling to the next, would benefit post-secondary education. This cannot happen, however, if those of us addressing these issues at the university level do not partner with our K–12 colleagues in meaningful professional development opportunities.

If we began to think of what we teach in college as both the culminating experiences of a lifetime of learning and an entry to new learning contexts such as workplaces and graduate school, we believe that a vertical curriculum allows the serving of two masters: providing disciplinary knowledge and teaching to transfer. In fact, English Studies generally has done very little to help ourselves by proving the value that our courses offer students. We assume that the ability to read a literary or theoretical text closely will transfer with the student, and that he or she will be able to read all texts closely and analytically. But where's the evidence? We also have boasted that writing—any kind of writing—will improve students' abilities to write in other courses, that learning MLA style will help them transition to APA or CBE style, that writing a killer personal narrative will help them write a lab report. As we discussed in the last section, writing studies is finally beginning to empirically investigate that claim, and as we alluded to in previous sections, the evidence suggests that a reframing of high school ELA classes and first-year writing is in order.

The essential framework that seems to emerge across the various studies is genre analysis as a problem-solving activity. As Robert Schwegler argues, when required composition courses were created at the end of the nineteenth century, English studies had different understandings of reading and writing in which literature was an object of analysis, and writing was a universal skill that was not contextually bound (25). In other words, good writing was good writing was good writing. As we came to understand that writing in engineering, science, or history differed by varying degrees from writing a clear expository essay, some English departments and universities began creating writing across the curriculum (WAC) courses to give students experience writing the types of documents they would see in their disciplines and professions.

Our burgeoning understanding of knowledge transfer coupled with current genre theory, though, rightly complicates this idea of writing as a fixed set of skills that transfer from one context to another. In the field, we throw around the term "genre" and see it used frequently in writing program outcome statements. Yet, as Barbara Little Liu argues, many writing programs do not seem to acknowledge in their curriculum the complicated meaning of genre and the implications of rich understanding of genre theory (72–73). Several scholars in the field have contributed to a nuanced understanding of genre theory as it can be used to conceive of reframed writing programs (Miller; Bazerman; Carter; Devitt; Russell; Downs and Wardle; Wardle; Reiff and Bawarshi) and we refer readers to those sources.

A first-year writing program that acts vertically and teaches for transfer must consider a genre-based approach rooted in a writing across the curriculum practice as argued for by multiple stakeholders (see Chapter Three) and supported by the goals of the Common Core State Standards. It seems to us that there are two basic manifestations of such an approach. One manifestation is a more generalized notion of rhetorical genres that would emphasize helping writers to read in multiple genres, deconstruct and analyze multiple genres, and write either in these multiple genres or in more meta-cognitive ways about genres. Liu argues that writers would also inquire into "the political and ideological agendas of writing communities" (81) as they write to or react against expectations of genre. A second manifestation would be emphasis on writing across the disciplines in first-year composition. In this approach, composition courses would focus less (if at all) on the "expository" text, but would consider how arguments are constructed across disciplines, a la Wolfe, as mentioned in Chapter Three, and write in various disciplinary genres. Because it is impossible to teach students all possible genres, students would also need to learn about genre analysis as a problem-solving activity in order to transfer knowledge from one context to another.

Various machinations of a genre-based approach or WAC approach have been offered by Downs and Wardle, Wardle, Fishman and Reiff, and others working at the intersection of genre studies, writing studies, and transfer. We will not rehash those here, but we would like to offer the salient considerations supported by research, presented in this and previous chapters, of a vertical curriculum:

- Genre-analysis must be a central focus.
- Students must write about and/or write in a variety of genres beyond the expository essay.
- The curriculum provides readings in a variety of genres.
- The curriculum emphasizes and teaches meta-cognitive awareness, including self-reflection, to facilitate high-road transfer of knowledge.

- Assignments must build sequentially upon one another in meaningful ways to promote knowledge transfer.
- The curriculum and its pedagogies must be made transparent and explicit to students to reinforce knowledge transfer.

This approach (or these variations on an approach) calls us back to our foundation in rhetorical study. Basing a college-level writing curriculum upon the study of and writing in genres calls on us to stake the territory of genre, rhetoric, and writing as ours, certainly shared with other disciplines like speech communication, but certainly ours. It also calls upon us to re-evaluate the multiplicity of approaches to writing: Our content is not literary analysis, cultural critique, or the like except as they support our central concern of teaching rhetoric and genre. Often first-year writing courses are seen as divorced from content, but in fact, our content is rhetoric.

We recognize that such a transformation of first-year writing curriculum and a vertical alignment of K–college writing curriculum will not be easy in many cases. And, we are forever concerned about the movement toward accomplishing such transformation through assessment schemes that center on accountability and standardized testing instead of assessment as an iterative, collaborative teaching and learning practice. In our own experiences and those of other writing program administrators and department chairs, we know that there is often resistance by the faculty in English departments to a more capacious thinking of genre that expands beyond the literary or expository genre. Often, adjunct faculty who may be firmly grounded in literature, creative writing, or other rhetorical theories that do not align with a genre-based approach, staff first-year writing courses. In our own experience working with teaching assistants (TAs), for example, we have observed that they are often resistant to teaching any citation practice other than MLA, in part because it is the only citation style that they have ever used. TAs and adjuncts, having rarely written in other academic genres, lack the confidence to teach these genres, or possess little interest in doing so. This approach, then, takes many faculty outside of their comfort zones. These and other problems are not insurmountable, and we believe that a transformative writing curriculum will utilize the knowledge that students will bring to college with them from a Common Core curriculum, stretching them into academic success in college and beyond.

CHAPTER 5
TEACHING WRITING MATTERS

At its core, this book is about the competition to govern, measure, and exploit literacy as it has played out since 2006, the year we are using as our pivot point as we look backward and forward in order to make decisions about shaping the path ahead of us through local and national efforts. Perhaps most importantly, it is about asserting the primary role of teachers as powerful *sponsors of literacy* working through networks on numerous levels—a role that requires a renewed commitment to writing instruction and research in our kindergarten through college classrooms horizontally across the curriculum and vertically through grade levels.

In *Literacy in American Lives,* Deborah Brandt defines sponsors of literacy as:

> any agents, local or distant, concrete or abstract, who en-
> able, support, teach, and model, as well as recruit, regulate,
> suppress, or withhold, literacy—and gain advantage by it in
> some way. . . . Sponsors are a tangible reminder that literacy
> learning throughout history has always required permission,
> sanction, assistance, coercion, or, at a minimum, contact with
> existing trade routes. (19)

While it is clear that more stakeholders than ever can be counted among the sponsors of literacy, so, too, is it clear that teachers are still among the primary sponsors of literacy. Furthermore, it may be that the only way for teachers to be effective sponsors of literacy at this current moment is if we do a better job of finding ways to shape and control the trade routes over which literacy travels. By trade routes, we mean those networks of pathways and stoppages through which literacy does, or doesn't travel. Brandt's work becomes vitally important in this effort as she helps us understand how literacy trade routes have been largely seized and governed by private economic interests:

> Literacy is being sponsored in much different ways than it was
> in the past. Through most of its history, literacy was affili-
> ated with a few strong cultural agents—education, religion,
> local commerce. It tended to be learned in the same contexts
> in which it was intended to be practiced. Now, sponsors of
> literacy are more prolific, diffused, and heterogeneous. . . .
> Commercial sponsors abound. (197)

For example, as Brandt demonstrates, in the early days of America, the church was one trade route to literacy, as Sunday School was begun to teach poor children math and reading in addition to religious values. We would argue today that testing companies and deep-pocketed private foundations control the trade routes to an unprecedented degree, acting as both a conduit to (at its best) and blockade to (at its worst) literacy acquisition.

Looking back at 2006, we now realize we were caught up in the midst of a newly energized clash of sponsors: "These clashes typically are between long-standing residual forms of sponsorship [e.g., university writing programs writ large] and the new, between the lingering influence of literacy's conservative history and its pressure for change" (Brandt 193). Indeed, our book is a call to teachers at all levels to do what they can to shape existing and emerging trade routes in ways that maintain the importance of writing as a public good, not a private interest, in the service of educational equity and opportunity. Doing so requires at least five significant changes:

1. Providing time in the work day for teachers to engage with local and national networks

2. Allowing significant amounts of time during the work day for collaborative planning and problem solving in one's department or school with other teachers, and sharing this work at the state and national level not only through yearly conferences, but sustainable structures such as the National Writing Project

3. Renewing our commitment to principles and practices of shared governance

4. Continuing insistence that open access to research data and results be required of private companies and public educational organizations so that more stakeholders have a voice in assessing the results of a research project and a voice in actions that might follow

5. Demanding that our school districts, as well as state and federal governments, not cede their historical role in providing for the means and direction of our public education system to private testing companies and advocacy philanthropists

As we take stock of what we have learned from our research, the research of others, and emerging developments in writing studies, we are convinced more than ever that *the teaching of writing matters*. And, it matters that teachers of writing be involved in creating sustainable structures for change in the ongoing battle over literacy.

EMPOWERING SPONSORS

In 2011, asserting its traditional role as a sponsor, the U.S. Department of Education appointed twenty-eight education advocates, civil rights leaders, scholars, lawyers, and corporate leaders to its Equity and Excellence Commission. Their report was issued early in 2013. Like many who follow these issues, we expected this report to be more of the same—more competition, more charter schools, more testing, more privatization, more corporate sponsorship. Unexpectedly, the commission's report, *For Each and Every Child: A Strategy for Education Equity and Excellence*, advocates funding schools justly and equitably, providing well-qualified teachers in all schools, opening access to universal early childhood education, serving and supporting at-risk students and families in high poverty areas (including providing access to health care), and governing to promote excellence (The Equity and Excellence Commission). The Commission's five-point action strategy touches upon what we believe to be the opportunity that holds the most promise for empowering and engaging teachers as sponsors of literacy—meaningful professional development—although our version of professional development places teachers in a more active, authorial role than does that of the commission.

The report's introduction, excerpted below, echoes the same findings many of us have been struggling with for many years, and is one of the most powerful admissions that despite all of our reforms and all of our tests, little progress has occurred:

> In 1983, *A Nation at Risk* famously spoke of the "rising tide of mediocrity" that threatened our schools. Nearly 30 years later, the tide has come in—and we're drowning. Since that landmark report, we've had five "education presidents" and dozens of "education governors" who have championed higher standards, innovative schools, better teaching, rigorous curricula, tougher testing and other education reforms. And, to be sure, there has been important progress. Reading and math performance levels in our elementary schools, for example, have improved in recent years, as has mathematics performance in our middle schools. (14)

Note that, once again, writing does not even merit mention in this account. The commission goes on to state:

> Except in a few states, however, the incremental steps we have taken have not been enough to keep pace with the dramatic

improvement other nations have made in their school systems. Moreover, any honest assessment must acknowledge
that our efforts to date to confront the vast gaps in educational outcomes separating different groups of young Americans have yet to include a serious and sustained commitment
to ending the appalling inequities—in school funding, in
early education, in teacher quality, in resources for teachers
and students and in governance—that contribute so mightily
to these gaps. (14)

For the remainder of this chapter we'd like to focus on one very specific aspect of this commission's action plan—teacher quality—within the specific concerns of literacy. For us, the question is not simply, how do we improve teacher
quality at this moment in time. Rather, as we frame the question—because the
teaching of writing matters, and teachers of writing matter—we must ask how
teachers can now assert a primary role as sponsors of literacy who are enabled to
shape the trade routes along which literacy travels. For us, the answer lies not in
the hiring of more, better teachers for more, better money. Instead, the answer
lies in context-specific professional development work that empowers and engages teachers as sponsors of literacy in both local and national networks. And,
in spite of its critics (which sometimes includes us), we do believe that the new
Common Core State Standards can be a motivating force in this effort. As the
commission notes: "the recent formulation of Common Core State Standards
. . . provides a unique moment to leverage excellence and equity for all and to
build on efforts to foster critical thinking and problem-solving, creativity and innovation, and communication" (15). However, this will *only* be true if teachers,
beginning in kindergarten and through college, are empowered and engaged in
shaping the routes CCSS travels, instead of allowing corporate interests to reign
as cash-strapped states are lured into adopting questionable practices.

One such practice is the continued overreliance on standardized tests as the
basis of school reform. As we evidenced earlier, despite hundreds of years of testing that has little to show in the way of improved learning, we persist in using
them as a primary measure and motivator. Recently, this practice has shown
great potential to be even more detrimental to reform efforts due to the growing insistence on machine-graded scoring of writing. Current machine-graded
scoring of standardized tests of writing is purported to be aligned with CCSS,
but in fact is rooted in simplified prompts and short answer essays that can be
measured by machines on the most basic levels. Grand claims about the cost
savings and reliability of machine-graded scoring, as well as the willingness of
cash-strapped states to adopt these programs, are not new. Nor is the repeated

abandonment of these testing products when they fail in exactly the ways that literacy scholars predict they will fail. For example, in 2002, Indiana adopted ETS's E-rater scoring engine. They quickly realized its shortcomings:

> It couldn't reliably handle questions that required students to demonstrate knowledge from the curriculum. State testing officials tried making lists of keywords the software could scan for: in history, for example, "Queen Isabella," "Columbus," and "1492." But the program didn't understand the relationship between those items, and so would have given full credit to a sentence like, "Queen Isabella sailed 1,492 ships to Columbus, Ohio." Cost and time savings never materialized, because most tests also had to be looked at by human graders. (Goldstein)

In a recent and widely publicized study of the accuracy of machine-graded scoring of human writing, Mark Shermis (University of Akron) and Ben Hamner (Kaggle) compare the abilities of nine different scoring engines to rate student writing. These authors found that "overall, automated essay scoring was capable of producing scores similar to human scores for extended-response writing items with equal performance for both source-based and traditional writing genre" (2). But a close look at their study reveals significant problems not only with their analysis, but also with what they analyzed. In his critique of this study, Les Perelman identifies four main areas of concern, which we summarize here:

1. The use of differing scoring rules for human graders and machine graders, which brings into question the validity of results. The claims made by Shermis and Hamner are based on the resolved score (RS). Many of us are familiar with resolved scores. For example, in writing programs with an exit portfolio, two readers will score a portfolio, and if their scores are identical or adjacent (e.g., do not differ by more than 1 point on a 6 point scale), then the resolved score is determined by adding the two scores and dividing them by two. If the two scores differ by more than 1 point then a third reader is used to determine the RS. Shermis and Hamner, however, not only use scoring rules for human graders that are not in line with best practices, but also use different scoring rules for the machine graders, thus using two different variables in their comparison: Shermis and Hamner's "text uses the variable H1H2, the reliability between the two readers, as the measure for reader reliability, while the measure for machine performance is reliability between machine and the resolved score (RS)" (5). Perelman considers this to be the greatest problem with their study.

2. The lack of standardly expected statistical tests appropriate for the data. Without using commonly expected statistical tests, some results seem to be based more on "hunches" or inferences rather than on valid statistical measures of significance.

3. The failure to test the entire model for significance. Without doing so, there is little way to prove that machines didn't outperform humans simply by random chance or pure dumb luck.

4. The lack of consistency in what was actually being measured. Half of the data sets were not extended written response essays, but rather were one-paragraph responses. Further, four of the datasets were not designed to measure writing ability, but rather reading comprehension and literary analysis. The difference in the length of the samples and the fact that many were not designed to measure writing ability did not stop Shermis and Hamner from using them to make claims about the accuracy of machine graders to score writing ability.

Finally, Perelman concludes, not only do Shermis and Hamner fail to prove their conclusion, but rather, "the data support the assertion that human scorers performed more reliably than the machines on the longer traditional writing assignments" (3).

While there is much we find troubling about this research, what troubles us most about Shermis and Hamner's study in light of our work here is Perelman's last critique—much of the writing being analyzed involved one-paragraph responses—and many were not even tests of writing ability. Dumbing down of tests in this way is required because machines are not yet capable of accurately assessing the types of complex writing we expect of our students. This dumbing down of tests in order to meet the machines present capabilities is akin to the narrowing of the curriculum that was a disastrous result of NCLB. Most importantly, much like the mystery that surrounds the data used for the analysis presented in the widely publicized book *Academically Adrift* that we critiqued in Chapter One, Shermis and Hamner's data is also a closely guarded secret. In situations where research results are used to inform practices as important as the implementation and assessment of the Common Core State Standards, we should insist upon this data being made readily available to other researchers for analysis so that it can be examined closely and debated in the field.

We have said elsewhere and say again that we are not staunch opponents of standardized tests, but we do oppose their current use as primary indicators of student learning as well as faculty achievement. Further, we *are* staunch opponents of dumbing down curricula to meet the limitations of standardized tests and the dumbing down of standardized tests so that they can be scored by machines. If CCSS is to have a chance at succeeding in raising the bar for writing across the curriculum, then we must insist on practices that lead to embracing the complexity of the CCSS, not altering them in the name of cheap and easy tests. Of course, the original intent of the CCSS is exactly the opposite: To provide national standards that present a robust picture of student achievement by setting ambitious but achievable goals. The CCSS itself, in fact, includes performance-based tasks for writing across the curriculum, tasks that would be difficult to leave to a machine-grader and nearly impossible to shrink to a one-paragraph response.

Standardized tests of writing do not have to lead to a narrowing of the curriculum or to writing assignments designed to meet the limitations of machine-graded scoring. If we look at the sample performance tasks, we see rich writing prompts across the curriculum that can be used to measure depth and breadth of knowledge as well as writing. For example, the CCSS suggest the following as a sample performance task for English Language Arts information texts for grades 6–8[1]:

> Students *trace* the line of *argument* in Winston Churchill's
> "Blood, Toil, Tears, and Sweat" address to Parliament and
> *evaluate* his specific claims and opinions *in the text, distin-*
> *guishing* which *claims* are supported by *facts, reasons, and*
> *evidence,* and which *are not.* (93)

For students in grades 9–10, a sample performance indicator for fiction, poetry, and drama suggests this prompt:

> Students *analyze how* the Japanese film maker Akira Kurosawa
> in his film *Throne of Blood draws on and transforms Shake-*
> *speare's play Macbeth* in order to develop a similar plot set in
> feudal Japan. (121–22).

The CCSS also support writing across the curriculum, as can be seen in the prompt for grades 9–12 in history/social sciences, sciences, mathematics, and technical subjects:

> Students *cite specific textual evidence* from Annie J. Cannon's
> "Classifying the Stars" to *support their analysis* of the scientific
> importance of the discovery that light is composed of many
> colors. Students *include in their analysis precise details* from
> the text (such as Cannon's repeated use of the image of the
> rainbow) to buttress their explanation. (138)

These performance tasks from the CCSS require students to demonstrate complex mastery of literacy—examining argumentative claims, working across genres and disciplines, and doing so in both reading and writing. To reduce these performance tasks to machine-gradable, short-answer summative assessments would largely undermine the laudable goals of CCSS.

EMPOWERING AND ENGAGED PROFESSIONAL DEVELOPMENT

In working to understand how to improve teacher quality, the Department of Education's Equity and Excellence Commission examined how other nations ensure teaching quality. Their report points out that unlike the United States, teacher training in high-performing countries is based on engagement with common instructional materials that support high-level national standards (22). In *Professional Learning in the Learning Profession: A Status Report on Teacher Development in the U.S. and Abroad*, Linda Darling-Hammond, Ruth Chung Wei, Alethea Andree, Nikole Richardson, and Stelios Orphanos discuss some of these differences:

> In most European and Asian countries, instruction takes up less than half of a teacher's working time (NCTAF, 1996, and OECD, 2007). The rest of teachers' working time—generally about 15 to 20 hours per week—is spent on tasks related to teaching like preparing lessons, marking papers, meeting with students and parents, and working with colleagues. Most planning is done in collegial settings, in the context of subject matter departments, grade level teams, or the large teacher rooms where teachers' desks are located to facilitate collective work.
>
> By contrast, U.S. teachers generally have from 3 to 5 hours a week for lesson planning, usually scheduled independently rather than jointly with colleagues (NCTAF, 1996). U.S. teachers also average far more net teaching time in direct contact with students (1,080 hours per year) than any other member of the Organization for Economic Cooperation and Development (OECD). By comparison, the OECD average is only 803 hours per year for primary schools and 664 hours per year for upper secondary schools (OECD, 2007). U.S. teachers spent about 80% of their total working time teaching students as compared to about 60% for teachers in these other nations, who thus have much more time to plan and learn together, and to develop high-quality curriculum and instruction. (20)

Parts of this description ring true for tenure-track professors in the United States as many of us lack the common spaces and institutional support for on-going, systematic professional development of our teaching. More troubling is that when it comes to non-tenure-track faculty, many of whom teach five or more writing classes each semester, this is an increasingly apt description of their working conditions. In fact, we would not be surprised to learn that most college writing instructors spend more than 85 percent of their time teaching students and even less time than their K–12 counterparts engaged in professional development. Thus, in our discussion below we abstract beyond K–12 classrooms to include structural changes needed at the college level as well.

As the Equity and Excellence Commission asserts: "Professional development must be embedded in the work day, deepen and broaden teacher knowledge, be rooted in best practice, allow for collaborative efforts, be aligned to the Common Core State Standards and provide the supports, time and resources to enable teachers to master new content, pedagogy and learning tools and incorporate them in their practice" (23). Of course, this general advice must be put into practice in ways that lead to improved student learning.

We usually equate improved student learning with improved teacher quality. And while this equation isn't false, the steps we follow in establishing this equation too often are. For example, as Carrie Leana, a professor of organizational management at the University of Pittsburgh, explains, we've come to believe that the keys to reforming our schools are identifying the most high-achieving teachers and using them as models that others should emulate, hiring outside consultants or identifying coaches, positioning principals as instructional leaders who, "in the language of business, . . . is a line manager expected to be a visible presence in the classroom, ensuring that teachers are doing their jobs." The problem with these beliefs is that while sometimes they can be helpful, there is considerable research showing that this approach alone is relatively ineffective. Leana's research provides evidence that if student learning is to show marked improvement *that is sustainable over time,* "schools must also foster what sociologists label 'social capital'—the patterns of interactions among teachers."

A growing body of research on effective professional development reveals that it is most often rooted in strong teacher networks with high levels of social capital. Indeed, as we argue for writing instruction that is positioned horizontally across the curriculum and vertically through grade levels, we know that this can only be successful in schools where structures exist that support high degrees of social capital among teachers. As Leana argues, when we look at a teacher's social capital, we are asking not only what does an individual teacher know that leads to her success, but also, how does she know it. In other words, how has she gained this knowledge? Where does she turn for new knowledge and advice when faced with new situations? The research of Leana and her colleagues shows that:

> When a teacher needs information or advice about how to do her job more effectively, she goes to other teachers. She turns far less frequently to the experts and is even less likely to talk to her principal. Further, when the relationships among teachers in a school are characterized by high trust and frequent interaction—that is, when social capital is strong—student achievement scores improve.

For example, in a study of 1,000 fourth and fifth grade teachers from 130 elementary schools in New York City, Leana and her colleagues wanted to find out if social capital is a significant predictor of student gains in math. Their results revealed that students showed higher gains in math when their teachers had higher levels of social capital, that is, "If a teacher's social capital was just one standard deviation higher than the average, her students' math scores increased by 5.7 percent."

Leana's study, as well as others, verifies a practice that permeates much of our professional literature, although often from an anecdotal perspective. That is, what may matter most is the networks that teachers build, formally or informally, in support of professional development and improved student learning. It is these same types of networks writing faculty must build in order to become positive sponsors of literacy, helping to shape the trade routes along which it travels. Formal communities like Bread Loaf, National Writing Project, Teaching and Learning Network, Learning Forward, ReadWriteThink, and the National Council of Teachers of English and their state affiliates can provide teachers with opportunities for professional development that are more than a collection of "Monday morning" worksheets. These venues provide teachers the opportunity to write, to learn, and to participate as active teacher scholars in their own professional development through both local and national networks. Time must be made in the work day of writing teachers to engage in these professional development opportunities.

Likewise, teachers must assert their role in the shared governance of our educational institutions—helping to make decisions with administrators about teaching and learning initiatives. As Gary Olson reminds us: "True shared governance attempts to balance maximum participation in decision making with clear accountability. . . . Genuine shared governance gives voice (but not necessarily ultimate authority) to concerns common to all constituencies as well as to issues unique to specific groups." But shared governance can only be effective if lines of communication are clear and open, again highlighting the need to make time for such activities during the work day. And, as we expand these opportunities we must engage in research that can determine the most successful structures for sustainable professional development. For example, one of the things we want to know as teacher-scholars is if teachers can gain social capital from both distant and immediate networks, if there are differences in what can be gained, if our professional conferences can do a better job at supporting these networks, and what role collective empirical research can play in increased engagement and improved learning across the curriculum.

While the work of Leana and her colleagues is somewhat unique in its focus on social capital, viewed from another perspective it is also simply one more significant piece of the growing body of research showing the value of effective professional development to improved student learning and achievement. For example, in Linda Darling-Hammond's et al. report on the status of professional development in the United States and high-achieving countries around the world, the researchers conducted a meta-analysis of 1,300 research studies and evaluation reports, and concluded that student achievement can be significantly improved through substantial professional development that ranges from 30–100 total hours, and is spread over six to twelve months: "intensive professional development efforts that offered an average of 49 hours in a year boosted student achievement by approximately 21 percentile points. Other efforts that involved a limited amount of professional development (ranging from 5 to 14 hours in total) showed no statistically significant effect on student learning" (9).

Despite these overwhelmingly positive results, when it comes to professional development, the United States lags far behind our high-achieving counterparts. For example, echoing the results of the research conducted by Leana and her colleagues, the authors of this report also did not find strong support for the effectiveness of coaches or hiring outside consultants in improving student learning and achievement. Further, among some of the most striking findings is that "Nationally, only 17 percent of [K–12] teachers reported a great deal of cooperative effort among staff members, and only 14 percent agreed that they had made conscious efforts to coordinate the content of courses" (25). While congeniality may be found in many schools, true collegiality is rare and can be difficult to sustain (Mindich and Lieberman). And, the difficultly in sustaining this type of work is in large part because in the United States teachers generally have three to five hours per week for tasks related to teaching, such as planning lessons, and this is most often done in isolation. In contrast, teachers in other countries, including high-achieving countries, allow for fifteen to twenty hours per week on tasks related to teaching including working with colleagues (Darling-Hammond, et al.). As Dan Mindich and Ann Lieberman make clear, collegiality is the cornerstone of professional development. They differentiate congeniality from collegiality by explaining that while congenial relationships are amiable they are often also conflict and risk-averse (18). "Collegial cultures on the other hand develop bonds of trust [and] provide a forum for reflection and honest feedback, for challenging disagreement and for accepting responsibility without assigning blame" (18). Building collegial cultures takes time our teachers are seldom given.

When it comes specifically to literacy, in "What Teachers Need," Darling-Hammond tells us that research presented by the National Center for Literacy Education (NCLE) confirms: "77% of educators, principals, and librarians agreed that developing student literacy is one of the most important responsibilities they have." Despite this finding, the same research reveals that only 32 percent of the respondents frequently create lessons together or reflect on whether or not a lesson worked, only twenty-one percent have time to review student work with each other on a frequent basis, only fourteen percent frequently receive formal feedback from peers, and only ten percent observe the teaching of others on a frequent basis. During the busy workaday of the school week and, it would seem, even at mandatory "School Improvement Days," little time is dedicated to reflection and collaboration among teachers—especially the types of collegial cultures that can lead to improved practices.

How might we develop collegial cultures that further empower and engage professional development? A multi-year study, "Professional Development in the United States: Trends and Challenges," published by Learning Forward and the Stanford Center for Opportunity Policy in Education, and funded by the Bill and Melinda Gates Foundation, is leading the way in answering this question. We have referenced reports from this study in a few sections of this book. At this point we focus on the seven standards for professional learning communities that grew out of the work of Dan Mindich and Ann Leiberman for this study. Professional learning that increases educator effectiveness and results for all students:

1. Occurs within learning communities committed to continuous improvement, collective responsibility, and goal alignment
2. Requires skillful leaders who develop capacity, advocate, and create support systems for professional learning
3. Requires prioritizing, monitoring, and coordinating resources for educator learning
4. Uses a variety of sources and types of student, educator, and system data to plan, assess, and evaluate professional learning

5. Integrates theories, research, and models of human learning to achieve its intended outcomes

6. Applies research on change and sustains support for implementation of professional learning for long-term change

7. Aligns its outcomes with educator performance and student curriculum standards

Exactly how a professional learning community might be operationalized following these standards is dependent on our specific contexts, and as our research enters its next phase, we look forward to identifying and developing local models for writing teachers.

Once in place, just what should empowered and engaged professional development opportunities position us to achieve as sponsors of literacy? We believe that they will allow us to do just what research on best practices, our individual experiences, and professional organizations such as the NCTE and CCCC believe we should be doing. They will lead us to a fuller realization of the many policy statements our professional organizations issue. The current pace of technology and disruptive forces in education mean we are faced with new tools, new genres and subgenres, and new models of composing at a sometimes dizzying speed. We must both document and research these changes while simultaneously teaching them. The timing has never been more crucial for inventing a new responsive and effective writing curriculum in K–graduate school—one that once again places writing, and teachers of writing, in the role of agent. We can't do it alone. It must happen through an essential broadening of our networks and strengthening of our social capital both locally and nationally. This book opens the dialogue for such a movement.

NOTE

1. We have chosen representative examples from the CCSS. Similar examples can be found across all grade levels, K–12, varying appropriately, of course, in complexity and expectation by grade level.

WORKS CITED

"2002–2003 ACT National Curriculum Survey Report." *ACT.* 2004. Web. 13 Feb. 2013.

"ACT National Curriculum Survey 2012: English Language Arts." *ACT.* 2013. Web. 17 Mar. 2015

"About NSSE." *NSSE—National Survey of Student Engagement.* n.d. Web. 30 Oct. 2012

"About the Standards." *Common Core State Standards Initiative.* n.d. Web. 12 Mar. 2014.

"About the Study." *Stanford Study of Writing.* 2008. Web. 30 Sept. 2009.

Addison, Joanne, and Sharon James McGee. "Writing in High School, Writing in College: Research Trends and Future Directions." *College Composition and Communication* 62.1 (2010): 147–179. Print.

Anderson, Paul, Chris Anson, Bob Gonyea, and Chuck Paine. "Summary: The Consortium for the Study of Writing in College." Unpublished Paper. Conference of Writing Program Administrators 2009. Minneapolis, MN. Web. http://www.niu.edu/wac/philosophy/NSSE-CWPA-Survey.pdf.

Anson, Chris M., and L. Lee Forsberg. "Moving beyond the Academic Community: Transitional Stages in Professional Writing." *Written Communication* 7.2 (1990): 200–231. Print.

Applebee, Arthur. "Great Writing Comes Out of Great Ideas." *The Atlantic.* 27 September 2012. Web. 20 May 2013.

———. "Issues in Large-Scale Writing Assessment: Perspectives from the National Assessment of Educational Progress." *Journal of Writing Assessment* 3.2 (2007): 81–98. Print.

———. *Writing in the Secondary School: English and the Content Areas.* Urbana, IL: National Council of Teachers of English, 1981. Print.

Applebee, Arthur N., and Judith A. Langer. "The State of Writing Instruction in America's Schools: What Existing Data is Telling Us." *Center on English Learning and Achievement.* 2006. Web. 25 May 2013.

———. "What Is Happening in the Teaching of Writing?" *English Journal* 98.5 (2009): 18–28. Print.

Arum, Richard, and Josipa Roksa. *Academically Adrift: Limited Learning on College Campuses.* Chicago: University of Chicago Press, 2011. Print.

"Assignments Matter: Grant Opportunity." *National Writing Project.* 14 Aug. 2014. Web. 10 May 2015. http://www.nwp.org/cs/public/print/events/768?x-t=sites_eos.view.

Astin, Alexander W. "In 'Academically Adrift' Data Don't Back Up Sweeping Claim." *The Chronicle of Higher Education.* 14 Feb. 2011. Web. 20 Feb. 2011.

Bazerman, Charles. *Shaping Written Knowledge: The Genre and Activity of the Experimental Article in Science.* Madison: University of Wisconsin Press, 1988. Print.

Beaufort, Anne. *College Writing and Beyond: A New Framework for University Writing Instruction*. Logan, UT: Utah State UP. 2007. Print.

Berg, Irwin A., Graham Johnson, and Robert P. Larsen. "The Use of An Objective Test in Predicting Rhetoric Grades." *Educational and Psychological Measurement* 5.44 (1945): 429–435. Print.

Berliner, David C., and Bruce J. Biddle. *The Manufactured Crisis: Myths, Fraud and the Attack on America's Public Schools.* White Plains, NY: Longman. 1995. Print.

Berliner, David C., and Gene V Glass. *50 Myths and Lies that Threaten America's Public Schools: The Real Crisis in Education.* New York, NY: Teachers College Press. 2014. Print.

Bergmann, Linda S., and Janet Zepernick. "Disciplinarity and Transfer: Students' Perceptions of Learning to Write." *WPA: Writing Program Administration* 31.1–2 (2007): 124–149. Print.

Black, Paul J. *Testing, Friend or Foe? The Theory and Practice of Testing and Assessment.* London, Washington: Falmer Press, 1998. Print.

Bracey, G. *Reading Research: How to Avoid Getting Educationally Snookered.* Portsmouth, NH: Heinemann, 2006. Print.

Bracey, G. "The Bracey Report on the Condition of Public Education." *Boulder and Tempe: Education and the Public Interest Center & Education Policy Research Unit.* 2009. Web. 25 Mar. 2015.

Bracco, K. R., M. Dadgar, K. Austin, B. Klarin, M. Broek, N. Finkelstein, S. Mundry, and D. Bugler. *Exploring the Use of Multiple Measures for Placement into College-Level Courses: Seeking Alternatives or Improvements to the Use of a Single Standardized Test.* San Francisco: CA: WestEd, 2014. Print.

Brannon, Lil. "Public Spaces, Private Interests: Teaching Writing in a Global Economy." Unpublished paper. Conference on College Composition and Communication, 2011, Atlanta, GA. Print.

Brandt, Deborah. *Literacy in American Lives.* New York, NY: Cambridge University Press, 2008. Print.

Brereton, John. *The Origins of Composition Studies in the American College: 1875–1925.* Pittsburgh, PA: University of Pittsburgh Press, 1996. Print.

Britton, J. N., T. Burgess, N. Martin, A. McLeod, and H. Rosen. *The Development of Writing Abilities (11–18).* London: MacMillan Educational for the Schools Council, 1975. Print.

Bryant, Brian R., and Diane Pedroty Bryant. "Assessing the Writing Abilities and Instructional Needs of Students." *Handbook of Psychological and Educational Assessment of Children.* Ed. Cecil R. Reynolds and Randy W. Kampaus. New York, NY: Guilford Press, 2003. 419–437. Print.

Caldwell, Otis W., and S. A. Courtis. 1869–1947. *Then & Now In Education, 1845: 1928: a Message of Encouragement From the Past to the Present.* Yonkers-on-Hudson, NY: World Book Company, 1925. Print.

Cadenhead, Kenneth, and Richard Robinson. "Fisher's 'Scale-Book' An Early Attempt at Educational Measurement." *Educational Measurement: Issues and Practice* 6.4 (1987): 15–18. Print.

Carter, Michael. "Ways of Knowing, Doing, and Writing in the Disciplines." *College Composition and Communication* 58.3 (2007): 385–418. Print.

CCCC Committee on Assessment. "Writing Assessment: A Position Statement." *Conference on College Composition and Communication.* Nov. 2006, revised Mar. 2009. Web. 22 April 2013.

Chickering, A. W., and Z. F. Gamson. "Seven Principles for Good Practice in Undergraduate Education." *AAHE Bulletin* 39.7 (1989): 3–7. Print.

Chickering, A. W., and Z. F. Gamson (eds.). Applying the Seven Principles for Good Practice in Undergraduate Education. *New Directions for Teaching and Learning*, no. 47. San Francisco: Jossey-Bass, 1991. Print.

Chingos, Matthew. "Strength in Numbers: State Spending on K-12 Assessment Systems." *The Brookings Institution.* 29 Nov. 2012. Web. 18 Apr. 2015.

"CLA+ Overview." CLA+ Overview. *Council for Aid to Education.* n.d. Web. 09 May 2015. http://cae.org/participating-institutions/cla-overview/.

Clotfelter, C. T., H. F. Ladd, and J. Vigdor. "Who Teaches Whom? Race and the Distribution of Novice Teachers." *Economics of Education Review* 24.4 (2005): 377–392. Print.

Coleman, James, et al. *Equality of Educational Opportunity for All.* Washington, DC: US Department of Health, Education, and Welfare, 1966. ERIC Database. ED012275.

"Colorado Measures of Academic Success." *Colorado Department of Education.* March 2015. Web. 15 May 2015.

"Common Core State Standards for English Language Arts & Literacy in History/Social Studies, Science, and Technical Subjects Appendix B: Text Exemplars and Sample Performance Tasks." *Common Core State Standards Initiative.* n.d. Web. 12 Mar. 2014.

"Core to College." *Rockefeller Philanthropy Advisors.* n.d. Web. 20 Sept. 2013.

Crawford, P., S. Lang, W. Fink, R. Dalton, and L. Fielitz. "Comparative Analysis of Soft Skills: What Is Important for New Graduates." *Michigan State University and the University Industry Consortium* (2011): 1–24. Web. 17 Sept. 2013.

Cutler, Laura, and Steve Graham. "Primary Grade Writing Instruction: A National Survey." *Journal of Educational Psychology* 100.4 (2006): 907–919. Print.

Darling-Hammond, Linda, and Ruth Chung Wei, Alethea Andree, Nikole Richardson, and Stelios Orphanos. "Professional Learning in the Learning Profession: A Status Report on Teacher Development in the US and Abroad. Technical Report." National Staff Development Council. 2009. Web. 13 Apr. 2013.

Darling-Hammond, Linda. "What Teachers Need and Reformers Ignore: Time to Collaborate." *The Washington Post.* n.p. 11 April 2013. Web. 13 Apr. 2013.

Davidson, Cathy. *Now You See It: How the Brain Science of Attention Will Transform the Way We Live, Work, and Learn.* New York: Viking Press, 2011. Print.

"Denver Writing Project Awarded Gates Foundation Grant to Develop Curricula for Local Teachers." *The Deans' Notes.* 3 Nov. 2011. Web. 16 Apr. 2013. http://clas.ucdenver.edu/deansNotes/issues/november32011.

Devitt, Amy. "Transferability and Genres." *The Locations of Composition*. Ed. Christopher J. Keller and Christian R. Weisser. Albany, NY: State U of New York P, 2007. 215–227. Print.

Dillon, Sam. "In Test, Few Students Are Proficient Writers." *New York Times* n.p. 3 Apr. 2008. Web. 1 Jan. 2015.

———. "Scholar's School Reform U-Turn Shakes Up Debate." *New York Times* n.p. 3 Mar. 2010. Web. 13 May 2013.

Downs, Doug, and Elizabeth Wardle. "Teaching about Writing, Righting Misconceptions: (Re)visioning 'First-year Writing' as "Introduction to Writing Studies." *College Composition and Communication* 58.4 (2007): 552–584. Print.

Elbow, Peter. "The War Between Reading and Writing: And How to End It." *Rhetoric Review* 12.1 (1993): 5–24. Print.

The Equity and Excellence Commission. *For Each and Every Child: A Strategy for Education Equity and Excellence*. Alexandria, VA: US Department of Education, Feb. 2, 2013. Web. 3 Jan. 2013.

"The Federal Role in Education." *U.S. Department of Education*. 13 Feb. 2012. Web. 29 Oct. 2014.

Finkelstein, N. D., B. Klarin, M. Olson, K. Austin, M. Dadgar, S. Mundry, and D. Bugler. "Core to College evaluation: Implementing the Common Core State Standards: Articulating Course Sequences across K–12 and Higher Education Systems." San Francisco, CA: WestEd, 2013.

Fishman, Jenn, and Mary Jo Reiff. "Taking it on the Road: Transferring Knowledge about Rhetoric and Writing across Curricula and Campuses." *Composition Studies* 39.2 (2011): 121–144. Print.

"Framework for Success in Postsecondary Writing." Council of Writing Program Administrators (CWPA), the National Council of Teachers of English (NCTE), and the National Writing Project (NWP). *Writing Program Administrators*. Jan. 2011. Web. 21 Apr. 2015. http://wpacouncil.org/framework.

Gallagher, Christopher W. "Being There: (Re)Making the Assessment Scene." *College Composition and Communication* 62.3 (2011): 450–476. Print.

———. "Believe it: NCLB-Style Accountability Extends to Higher Education." *Fair Test: The National Center for Fair and Open Testing*. 19 June 2007. Web. 13 June 2013.

Garcia, Nelson. "Students Refuse to Take Standardized Tests." 9 News. Denver, CO, 13 Nov. 2014. Television. http://www.9news.com/story/news/education/2014/11/13/students-refuse-to-take-standardized-test/18973697.

George Mason University. "Faculty Survey on Student Writing." Writing Assessment Group. George Mason University. n.d. Web. 30 Sept. 2012.

Goldstein, Dana. "Machines Shouldn't Grade Student Writing—Yet." *Slate*. 9 May 2012. Web. 10 May 2012.

Gamoran, Adam, and Daniel A. Long. *Equality of Educational Opportunity A 40 Year Retrospective*. Netherlands: Springer, 2007.

Giltrow, Janet. "Meta-genre." *The Rhetoric and Ideology of Genre*. Ed. Richard Coe, Lorelei Lingard, and Tatiana Teslenko. Cresskill, NY: Hampton Press, 2002. 187–205.

Glass, Gene V. "Meta-analysis at 25." *Gene V Glass webpage*. Arizona State University. Jan. 2000. Web. 30 Sept. 2012.

Graham, Steve, Debra Mckeown, Sharlene Kiuhara, and Karen R. Harris. "Meta-analysis of Writing Instruction for Students in Elementary Grades": Correction to Graham Et Al. (2012)." *Journal of Educational Psychology* 104.4 (2012): 879–896. Print.

Graham, Steve, and Dolores Perin. "A Meta-Analysis of Writing Instruction for Adolescent Students." *Journal of educational psychology* 99.3 (2007): 445. Print.

Graham, Steve, and Dolores Perin. "Writing Next: Effective Strategies to Improve Writing of Adolescents in Middle and High Schools. A Report to Carnegie Corporation of New York." *Alliance for Excellent Education* (2007). Print.

Grissom, J. A. "Can Good Principals Keep Teachers in Disadvantaged Schools? Linking Principal Effectiveness to Teacher Satisfaction and Turnover in Hard-to-Staff Environments." *Teachers College Record* 113 (2011): 2552–2585. Print.

Guisbond, Lisa, with Monty Neill and Bob Schaeffer. "NCLB's Lost Decade for Educational Progress: What Can We Learn from this Policy Failure?" *Fair Test: The National Center for Fair and Open Testing*. January 2012. Web. 10 May 2015.

Hall, Cassie. *'Advocacy Philanthropy' and the Public Policy Agenda: The Role of Modern Foundations in American Higher Education*. Thesis. Claremont Graduate University, 2011. UMI (1500712). Print.

Hanson, Allan F. *Social Consequences of the Examined Life*. Berkeley, CA: University of California Press, 1992. Print.

Haswell, Richard H. "Methodologically Adrift." *College Composition and Communication* 63.3 (2012): 487–91. Print.

Haynes, Mariana. "On the Path to Equity: Improving the Effectiveness of Beginning Teachers." Alliance for Excellent Education. July 2014. Web. 25 Dec. 2015. http://all4ed.org/wp-content/uploads2014/07/PathToEquity.pdf.

Hillegas, Milo B. "A Scale for the Measurement of Quality in English Composition by Young People." *Teachers College Record*. Sept. 1912: 1–54. Web. 25 Oct. 2015.

Hillocks, George, Jr. *The Testing Trap: How State Writing Assessments Control Learning*. Teachers College Press. New York, NY: 2002. Print.

Hess, Rick. "The Common Core Kool-Aid." Rick Hess's Straight Up Blog. *Education Week*. 30 November 2012. Web. 12 Dec. 2012.

Hiss, William C., and Valerie W. Frank. Defining Promise: Optional Standardized Testing Policies in American College and University Admissions. Rep. *National Association for College Admission Counseling*. 2 May 2014. Web. 15 Apr. 2015.

Hollis, E. V. *Philanthropic Foundations and Higher Education*. New York: Columbia University Press: 1938. Print.

"How Standardized Tests Shape—and Limit—Student Learning." *Council Chronicle* 24.2 (2014): 1–3. Print.

Hughes, Gerunda B., et al. "A Study of the Alignment between the NAEP Mathematics Framework and the Common Core State Standards for Mathematics (CCSS-M)." *American Institutes for Research*. 2013. Web. 10 May 2015.

Illinois State Board of Education. "PARCC Assessment FAQs." Illinois State Board of Education. January 2015. Web. 6 June 2015.

James R. Squire Office of Policy Research. "First Year Writing: What Good Does it Do?" *National Council of Teachers of English*. 2013. Web. 24 June 2014. http://www.ncte.org/library/NCTEFiles/Resources/Journals/CC/0232-nov2013/CC0232 Policy.pdf.

Johnson, J. Paul, and Ethan Krase. "Articulating Claims and Presenting Evidence: A Study of Twelve Student Writers, From First-Year Composition to Writing Across the Curriculum." *The WAC Journal* 23 (2012): 31–48. Web.

Johnson, Franklin. "The Hillegas-Thorndike Scale for Measurement of Quality in English Composition by Young People. *The School Review* 21.1 (1913): 39–49. Web. 25 Oct. 2013.

Jones, Lyle V. "A History of the National Assessment of Educational Progress and Some Questions About Its Future." *Educational Researcher* 25.7 (1996): 15–22. Print.

Kendall, John. *Understanding Common Core State Standards*. Alexandria, VA: ASCD, 2011.

"Kinds of Writing." Stanford Study of Writing. 2008. Web. 30 Sept. 2009.

Klein, Joel, and Condoleezza Rice. "U.S. Education Reform and National Security." *Council on Foreign Relations*. 12 Mar. 2012. Web. 9 May 2015.

Klein, Stephen, et al. "The Collegiate Learning Assessment Facts and Fantasies." *Evaluation Review* 31.5 (2007): 415–439. Print.

Lane, David M., and Frederick L. Oswald. "Academically Adrift, Critical Thinking, Arun and Roksa, Limited Learning." Academically Adrift, Critical Thinking, Arun and Roksa, Limited Learning. n.p., n.d. Web. 9 May 2015.

Laird, Thomas F., Michael J. Schwarz, Rick Shoup, and George Kuh. "Disciplinary Differences in Faculty Members' Emphasis on Deep Approaches to Learning." Annual Meeting of the Association for Institutional Research. Chicago. 14–18 May 2005. Web. 8 Mar. 2010.

Laird, Thomas F., Rick Shoup, and George D. Kuh. "Measuring Deep Approaches to Learning Using the National Survey of Student Engagement." Annual Meeting of the Association for Institutional Research. Chicago. 14–18 May 2005. Web. 8 Mar. 2010.

Layton, Lyndsey. "How Bill Gates Pulled off the Swift Common Core Revolution." *The Washington Post*. 7 June 2014. Web. 18 Apr. 2015.

Leana, Carrie R. "The Missing Link in School Reform." *Stanford Social Innovation Review*. Fall 2011. Web. 17 June 2013.

Lenhart, Amanda, Sousan Arafeh, Aaron Smith, and Alexandra Macgill. "Writing, Technology and Teens." *Pew Internet and American Life Project and National Commission on Writing*. 24 Apr. 2008. Web. 19 June 2013.

Licklider, Mary M. "Are Today's Students Better Writers?" *The English Journal* 81 (1992): 34–39. Print.

Light, Richard. *Making the Most of College*. Cambridge, MA: Harvard University Press, 2001. Print.

"Literacy Design Collaborative, Inc." *Bill and Melinda Gates Foundation*. July 2013. Web. 10 May 2015.

Liu, Barbara Little. "More Than the Latest PC Buzzwords for Modes: What Genre Theory Means to Composition." *The Outcomes Book: Debate and Consensus after the WPA Outcomes Statement.* Ed. Susanmarie Harrington, Keith Rhodes, Ruth Overman Fischer, Rita Malenczyk. Logan, UT: Utah State UP, 2005. Print.

"Longitudinal Study of Writing." *University of Denver University Writing Program.* n.d. Web. 10 May 2015.

Loveless, Tom. "Measuring Effects of the Common Core." *The Brookings Institution.* March 24, 2015. Web. 15 May 2015.

Mangan, Katherine. "Colleges Must Help Further the Goals of Common Core Standards, Report Says." *The Chronicle of Higher Education.* 22 July 2014. Web. 20 May 2015.

Mathison, Susan. "A Short History of Standardized Assessment and Standards-Based Educational Reform." *Defending Public Education.* Vol 4. Ed. David A. Gabbard, E. Wayne Ross. Greenwood Publishing, 2004. 3–14. Print.

Meacham, Jon. "What Will College Teach in 2025." *Time Magazine.* October 7, 2013. Print.

Melzer, Dan. "Assignments across the Curriculum: A Survey of College Writing." *Language and Learning Across the Disciplines* 6.1 (Jan. 2003): 86–110. Print.

Miller, Carolyn R. "Genre as Social Action." *Quarterly Journal of Speech* 70 (1984): 151–167. Print.

Mindich, Dan, and Ann Lieberman. "Building a Learning Community: A Tale of Two Schools." *Stanford Center for Opportunity Policy in Education.* 2012. Web. 22 Nov. 2013.

Mudgway, Douglas J. *William H. Pickering: America's Deep Space Pioneer.* Washington, DC: National Aeronautics and Space Administration, 2007. Print.

"'A Nation at Risk: The Imperative for Educational Reform:'A Report to the Nation and the Secretary of Education." *U.S. Department of Education.* April 1983. Web. 12 May 2013.

National Center for Education Statistics. *The Nation's Report Card: Reading 2009* (NCES 2010–458). Washington, DC: Institute of Education Sciences, U.S. Department of Education, 2009. Web. 12 Nov 2013.

National Center for Educational Statistics. *The Nation's Report Card: Writing 2011* (NCES 2012-470). Washington, DC: U.S. Department of Education, 2012. Web. 12 Nov 2013.

"NCTE-WPA White Paper on Writing Assessment in Colleges and Universities." *Council of Writing Program Administrators.* 2008. Web. 24 March 2014.

Nelms, Gerald, and Ronda Leathers Dively. "Perceived Roadblocks to Transferring Knowledge from First-Year Composition to Writing-Intensive Major Courses: A Pilot Study." *WPA: Writing Program Administration* 31.1 (2007): 214–240. Print.

National Commission on Writing. "The Neglected 'R': The Need for a Writing Revolution." *College Board.* 2003. Web. 28 Sept. 2009.

———. "Writing: A Powerful Message from State Government." *College Board.* 2005. Web. Feb. 2010.

————. "Writing: A Ticket to Work . . . or a Ticket Out: A Survey of Business Leaders." *College Board*. 2004. Web. 30 Sept. 2009.

————. "Writing and School Reform." *College Board*. 2006. Web. 28 Mar. 2014.

"Promoting Engagement for All Students: The Imperative to Look Within, 2008 Results." National Survey Student Engagement. Bloomington: Indiana U Center for Postsecondary Research, 2009. Web. 30 Sept. 2009.

Newkirk, Thomas. "Postscript: Speaking Back to the Common Core." (A web chapter added to a originally print-based book in 2013). *Holding onto Good Ideas in a Time of Bad Ones*. Portsmouth, NH: Heinemann, 2009. Web. 13 Dec. 2013.

Odell, Lee, and Dixie Goswami, eds. *Writing in Nonacademic Settings*. New York: Guilford, 1985. Print.

Olson, Gary. "Exactly What is 'Shared Governance.'" *The Chronicle of Higher Education*. 23 July 2009. Web. 20 Jan. 2014.

Ost, Ben. "How Do Teachers Improve? The Relative Importance of Specific and General Human Capital." *American Economic Journal: Applied Economics* 6.2 (2015): 127–151. Print.

"Overview | Literacy Design Collaborative." Literacy Design Collaborative. n.d. Web. 10 May 2015.

Parker, Flora E., and S. A. Courtis. "The Value of Measurements: I. The Measurement of Composition in English Classes: II. The Uses of the Hillegas Scale." *The English Journal* 8.4 (1919): 203–217. Web. 28 October 2013.

Paris, David C. "Catalyst for Change: The CIC/CLA Consortium." *Council of Independent Colleges*. 2011. Web. 12 March 2013.

Patterson, J. P., and David Duer. "High School Teaching and College Expectations in Writing and Reading." *English Journal* 95.3 (2006): 81–87. Print.

Perkins, D. N., and Gavriel Salomon. "Teaching for Transfer." *Educational Leadership*. 46.1 (1988): 22–32. Print.

Perelman, Les. "Critique (Ver. 3.4) of Mark D. Shermis & Ben Hammer, 'Contrasting State-of-the-Art Automated Scoring of Essays: Analysis.'" http://dl.dropbox.com /u/82100708/Critique_of_Shermis_Hammer_Paper_Ver_3_4_complete_final.pdf.

————. "WAC Revisited: You Get What You Pay For." *The Writing Instructor*. Dec. 2011. Web. 15 May 2015.

Perez-Péña, Richard. "Trying to Find a Measure for How Well Colleges Do." *New York Times*. 7 April 2012. Web. 10 April 2012.

Peters, Joey. "State Denies Protest Of Common Core-aligned Testing Contract" *Santa Fe Reporter*. 3 July 2014. Web. 30 Sept. 2014.

Phillips, Gary W. "Statement on Long Term Trend Writing NAEP." *National Center for Educational Statistics*, 11 April 2000. Web. 13 Mar. 2014.

Ravitch, Diane. *The Death and Life of the Great American School System: How Testing and Choice Are Undermining Education*. New York: Basic Books, 2010. Print.

————. "My View of the Common Core Standards." *Diane Ravitch's Blog*. 9 July 2102. Web. 20 December 2012.

————. "NCLB: The Death Star of American Education." *Education Week* "Bridging the Differences Blog." 10 January 2012. Web.

Reiff, Mary Jo, and Anis Bawarshi. "Tracing Discursive Resources: How Students Use Prior Genre Knowledge to Negotiate New Writing Contexts in First-Year Composition." *Written Communication* 28.3 (2011): 312–337. Print.

Rich, Mokoto. "Delay Urged on Actions Tied to Tests by Schools." *New York Times.* 10 June 2014. Web. 1 May 2015.

Rivlin, Alice. "Measuring Performance in Education" in *The Measurement of Economic and Social Performance.* Ed. Milton Moss. National Bureau of Economic Research. 1973. 411–438. Print.

Rosenthal, Jack. "A Terrible Thing to Waste." *New York Times.* 31 July 2009. Web. 20 Mar. 2015.

Russell, David R. "Writing across the Curriculum in Historical Perspective: Toward a Social Interpretation." *College English* 52.1 (1990): 52–73. Print.

Schwegler, Robert A. "Curricular Development in Composition." *Coming of Age: The Advanced Writing Curriculum.* Ed. Linda K. Shamoon, Rebecca Moore Howard, Sandra Jamison, Robert A. Schewegler. Portsmouth, NH: Boynton/Cook, 2000. 25–31. Print.

"Secretary Duncan, Urban League President Morial to Spotlight Spotlight States Where Education Funding Shortchanges Low-Income, Minority Students." *U.S. Department of Education.* 13 Mar. 2015. Web. 25 Mar. 2015.

Seib, Gerald F. "In Crisis, Opportunity for Obama." *Wall Street Journal.* 21 Nov. 2008. Web. 20 April 2015.

Shannon, Patrick. "An Evidence Base for the Common Core." *Closer Readings of the Common Core.* Ed. Patrick Shannon. Portsmouth: Heinemann, 2013. 1–19. Print.

Shannon, Patrick, Anne Elrod Whitney, and Maja Wilson. "The Framing of the Common Core State Standards." *Language Arts* 91.4 (2014): 295–302. Print.

Shermis, Mark, and Ben Hamner "Contrasting State-of-the-Art Automated Scoring of Essays: Analysis." Unpublished Paper. http://www.scoreright.org/NCME_2012_Paper3_29_12.pdf.

Simon, Nicole S., and Susan Moore Johnson. "Teacher Turnover in High-Poverty Schools: What We Know and Can Do." Project on the Next Generation of Teachers. Harvard Graduate School of Education. August 2013. Web. 20 May 2015. http://isites.harvard.edu/fs/docs/icb.topic1231814.files/Teacher%20Turnover%20 in%20High-Poverty%20Schools.pdf.

Simon, Stephanie. "No Profit Left Behind." *Politico.* 15 Feb. 2015. Web. 18 Apr. 2015.

Skinnell, Ryan. "Harvard, Again: Considering Articulation and Accreditation in Rhetoric and Composition's History." *Rhetoric Review* 33.2 (2014): 95–112. Print.

Smit, David W. *The End of Composition Studies.* Carbondale, IL: Southern Illinois UP, 2004. Print.

Sommers, Nancy. "The Call of Research: A Longitudinal View of Writing Development." *College Composition and Communication* 60.1 (2008): 152–164. Print.

Sommers, Nancy, and Laura Saltz. "The Novice as Expert: Writing the Freshman Year." *College Composition and Communication* 56.1 (2004): 124–149.

Spilka, Rachel. "Influencing Workplace Practice: A Challenge for Professional Writing Specialists in Academia." *Writing in the Workplace: New Research Perspectives.* Ed.

Rachel Spilka. Carbondale: Southern Illinois UP, 1993. 207–19. Print.

Spellings Commission. *A Test of Leadership: Charting the Future of U.S. Higher Education*. Washington, DC: US Department of Education, 2006. Web. 12 Oct. 2012.

Strain, Margaret. "In Defense of a Nation: The National Defense Education Act, Project English, and the Origins of Empirical Research in Composition." *JAC* 25.3 (2005): 513–542. Print.

Strauss, Valerie. "Two More States Pull Out of Common Core." *Washington Post*. 5 June 2014. Web. 20 August 2014.

"Supporting English Language Learners: A Pocket Guide for State and District Leaders." American Institutes for Research. 6 Dec. 2012. Web. 30 March 2013.

"Supporting Instruction: Investing in Teaching." *Bill and Melinda Gates Foundation*. 2010. Web. 27 March 2013. http://www.gatesfoundation.org/highschools/Documents/supporting-instruction.pdf.

Thomas, Swain Charles. "The Hillegas Scale." *New England Association of Teachers of English*. Leaflet #104. 1913. Web. 12 October 2013.

Thorndike, Edward L. *Education: A First Book*. New York: Macmillan. 1912. Print.

Tienken, Christopher H., and Donald C. Orlich. *The School Reform Landscape: Fraud, Myth, and Lies* (Kindle Locations 553–559). Lanham, MD: Rowman and Littlefield Education, 22 Feb. 2013. Kindle Edition.

"To Create Teaching Models to Improve Writing Instruction." *National Writing Project*. 1 Nov. 2010. Web. 10 May 2015.

"VALUE Rubric Development Project." *Association of American Colleges and Universities*. n.d. Web. 4 June 2015.

Ward, A.W., and M. Murray-Ward. *Assessment in the Classroom*. Albany, NY: Wadsworth Publishing Company, 1999. Print.

Wardle, Elizabeth. "'Mutt Genres' and the Goal of FYC: Can We Help Students Write the Genres of the University?" *College Composition and Communication* 60.4 (2009): 765–789. Print.

———. "Understanding 'Transfer' from FYC: Preliminary Results of a Longitudinal Study." *WPA: Writing Program Administrator* 31.1/2 (2007): 65–85. Print.

Wei, Ruth Cheng, Linda Darling-Hammond, and Frank Adamson. "Professional Development in the United States: Trends and Challenges." Dallas, TX: National Staff Development Council, 2010. Print.

Washington, Sharon J. "Congress, Obama Cut Funding for National Writing Project." *National Writing Project*. 6 Mar. 2011. Web. 18 Apr. 2014.

"What is NCTE Saying About Assessment." *National Council of Teachers of English Rapid Response Assessment Task Force*. Urbana: National Council of Teachers of English. Web. 7 December 2014.

The White House. Office of the Press Secretary. Remarks by the President in State of Union Address. The Press Office, 25 Jan. 2011. Web. 20 Mar. 2015.

Whitehurst, Grover. "The Future of Test-Based Accountability." *Brookings Brief: The Brown Center Chalkboard*. Washington, DC: The Brookings Institution, 14 July 2015. Web. 25 Mar. 2015.

Wixson, K., S. Velencia, S. Murphy, and G. Phillips. "A Study of NAEP Reading and Writing Frameworks and Assessments in Relation to the Common Core State Standards in English Language Arts." *American Institutes for Research* (2013). Web. 9 Feb. 2014.

Wolfe, Christopher R. "Argumentation Across the Curriculum." *Written Communication* 28.2. (2011): 193–219. Print.

"Writing Now." A Policy Research Brief Produced by the National Council of Teachers of English. Urbana: National Council of Teachers of English, 2008. Web. 14 Mar 2014.

Yancey, Kathleen Blake. *Writing in the 21st Century: A Report from the National Council of Teachers of English*. Urbana: National Council of Teachers of English, 2009. Web. 3 February 2014.